Conquering Your Anger

By

Rick Carter Jr. Ph.D.

Conquering Your Anger

IBA Publishing
2424 SW 135th St
Oklahoma City, OK 73170

www.IBADirect.com
Hope4Addictions.com

All Scripture taken from the authorized King James Bible

ISBN: 978-1602084377

CONTENTS

"And he said, That which cometh out of the man, that defileth the man. For from within, out of the heart of men, proceed evil thoughts, adulteries, fornications, murders, Thefts, covetousness, wickedness, deceit, lasciviousness, an evil eye, blasphemy, pride, foolishness: All these evil things come from within, and defile the man."
~Mark 7:20-23

One

Where Does My Anger Come From?

Look on the internet for why people get angry and you will find a broad and incoherent list of reasons on thousands of websites. There doesn't seem to be any definitive list. Even on websites that seem to site studies and psychological research the results are random. In all the various ideas and lists a constant theme does seem to rise which is that most anger is the result of a broken expectation we had. An article on theguardian.com sites a number of studies but singles out one in particular called the frustration-aggression hypothesis which says, "we get angry when frustrated; when our desires, goals or expectations are thwarted."

Consider some of the specific topics on other lists like, driving complaints, work problems, marital conflicts and others most of these could be listed under a similar category that simply declares that I had an expectation that someone would behave a certain way and they didn't, this in turn made me angry. Let me interject then that in my estimation the majority of things that are listed as causing anger are directly related to broken expectations. Now I am not a psychologist, nor do I endorse the secular psychological views. I do however have three things that set me apart to write on this subject.

1. Most importantly, I am an avid student of the Bible.
2. I spent years of my life struggling with anger until finding a real answer to conquer it.

3.   I have a doctorate in Biblical Counseling.
I will be sharing with you tools that I use in personal counseling throughout the next couple chapters to help you understand and apply the truths that we will be discussing. I will also be giving you testimony of my personal experience as a help for making direct application of these truths. But I do want you to understand that all of these things are going to be based upon the direct application of the Bible.

Let me show you the relevance of the Bible on this topic. I just shared that a secular view of anger seems to indicate that broken expectations are the leading cause of anger. That reality is directly backed up by the Biblical narrative. As a matter of fact, if a person were to study all the instances of people getting angry in the Bible you would find 40 classifiable illustrations. That is, there are 40 places where enough discussion is given to categorize why an individual was angry.

Of these 18 times, their anger is directly attributable to a broken expectation. That represents 45% of the time that someone in the Bible got angry.

8 times, or 20% of the time their anger was because of their own pride being hurt. In these instances, the individual became angry because of a perceived offence against themselves.

5 times or 12.5% of the time it was because someone else acted prideful and it caused anger.

4 times or 10% of the time anger was the result of an injustice that was done to someone else.

The remaining direct illustrations of anger related to greed, betrayal, provocation and actually learning anger from being around an angry person.

This is a very complete list that summarizes a broad swath of what secular studies have also found by placing them in broader categories. My point is that the Bible already illustrated what causes anger and the same things that caused anger in Bible times are still applicable to us today. Additionally, the Bible gives answers for these issues by not only teaching directly how to deal with our own anger but how to deal with those around us who get angry. Inside the pages of this book, we are going to explore these answers and make direct application to help us conquer anger.

In order to begin this process let's consider the leading cause of anger by every measure, namely, broken expectations. Since it is true that this is the number one cause of anger I want you to consider with me an inconvenient reality. Anger is not something that is done to you, it is not something that happens to you as though it were outside of you and forcing you to be angry. Anger comes from inside of you, it may be that outside pressures reveal it, but it is only revealing what is already a problem inside of your heart. Anger is often revealed when pressure is applied in our lives, but the pressure is only revealing the flaw that is already there.

Jesus taught this very thing in Mark 7:20-23 which says, "And he said, That which cometh out of the man, that defileth the man. For from within, out of the heart of men, proceed evil thoughts, adulteries, fornications, murders, Thefts, covetousness, wickedness, deceit, lasciviousness, an evil eye, blasphemy, pride, foolishness: All these evil things come from within, and defile the man." The source of our problems are not those things that happen to us, but how we respond to them. Someone wisely said, "the heart of every problem is a problem of the heart." One event can produce many different responses. If there is a wreck on Western Avenue in front of our church one person might respond in anger to the situation while another might respond in gratitude that there was no one hurt, or they weren't hurt worse. The event was the same for both, but the response is not the result of the event, it is the result of what is in each heart.

Circumstances never cause our emotional consequences; the consequences are always the result of the beliefs that we have. The first thing that we must address then in relationship to anger is the wrong beliefs that we have concerning the number one cause for anger which is broken expectations. Consider with me for a minute then what the Bible says about expectations.

Jeremiah 17:5-6 gives us an alarming warning about expectations by saying, "Thus saith the LORD; Cursed be the man that trusteth in man, and maketh flesh his arm, and whose heart departeth from the LORD. For he shall be like the heath in the desert, and shall not see when good cometh; but shall inhabit the parched places in the wilderness, in a salt land and not inhabited."

The term here, "trust in man" is a Bible way of saying putting your expectation in men. The result shown here is that when you put your expectation or trust in men you also put yourself under a curse. The curse is that your expectation is going to be broken. People fail. The humorist Dave Berry says, "The one thing that unites all human beings, regardless of age, gender, religion, economic status, or ethnic background, is that, deep down inside, we all believe that we are above-average drivers." Of course, most people who deal with anger on a regular basis find other drivers infuriating. When you get in a car and have the unrealistic expectation that other drivers are going to obey the laws and be courteous you have put yourself under a curse. It is always important to remember that the law of averages demands that half of the people on the road are below average drivers. Having an expectation otherwise condemns you to anger.

The same reality is to be expected in every other part of life. Many times, unfortunately, we treat strangers better than those who are the closest to us and we actually love the most. The reason for that is because we put much higher expectations on those we know. Your parents, spouse, children, boss, employees, co-workers, neighbors and friends are all targets for your bad expectations. Having the wrong expectation that they will never fail, forget, or even just choose something other than we want is the source of much anger. Let me shock you possibly, it is not the responsibility of every person in your life to do what you want all the time or to please you. Your personal happiness is your own responsibility and if you are going to conquer anger in your life you must free everyone else from the chains of your expectations on them.

No one in your life is responsible for your anger but you. No one in your life is responsible for your happiness but you. Free them, give them permission to be human, give them permission to fail. This not only frees them from the pressure that you have put on them, but it will free you from the chains of anger. Let me clarify one very important thing that I always get asked at this point. The question is, "shouldn't I have some expectations? I should still expect my spouse to be faithful and my children to obey, shouldn't I?"

Let's distinguish between our desire for someone to do right and our expectation that they will. To do this let's ask a question about God and expectations. Did God expect men to sin after creation, or was He caught off guard by Adam's choice to sin? God gave Adam one commandment in the garden, don't eat of the tree of the knowledge of good and evil, Adam broke the only commandment that He had, did God expect that? The answer to that question is yes, God did expect that. The reason we know God's expectation is that the Bible says in 1 Peter 1:18-21 "Forasmuch as ye know that ye were not redeemed with corruptible things, as silver and gold, from your vain conversation received by tradition from your fathers; But with the precious blood of Christ, as of a lamb without blemish and without spot: Who verily was foreordained before the foundation of the world, but was manifest in these last times for you, Who by him do believe in God, that raised him up from the dead, and gave him glory; that your faith and hope might be in God."

God prepared for man's redemption before He created the world. That tells us that man's sin was not a surprise to God. Let's ask the alternate question, Did God desire for men to sin? The answer to that is a clear and definite, no. God told Adam not to sin, His desire was that men not sin and remain in a state of sinless perfection where their relationship with Him would not be hindered by rebellion. His desire for our fellowship should not be confused with His expectation for our sin however.

The same is true for Christians today. Does God expect us to sin? Yes, in 1 John 1:9 it says, "If we confess our sins, he is faithful and just to forgive us our sins, and to cleanse us from all unrighteousness." Did you notice the phrasing, if we confess our sin, not if we sin? Sin is actually the expectation of that verse, it is confession that is not expected. Again, does God desire us to sin? NO, as Paul says in Romans 6:1-2, "What shall we say then? Shall we continue in sin, that grace may abound? God forbid. How shall we, that are dead to sin, live any longer therein?" God's desire is for

5

us to stay away from sin, but He does not have an unreal expectation that we will never sin.

Let me define this for you just a little bit more, sin is defined in the Bible as breaking God's commandments. When we break God's law we are guilty of transgression and as such reap the penalty of sin which the Bible says is death, or eternal separation from God. This means that sin causes men death and sorrow. God loves us and wants the best for us, He wants us to live with Him forever in peace. Thus, when we sin God is disappointed for us because he knows the consequences and how they affect us. Yet because God expected us to sin He has never been disappointed in us, His love for us simply causes Him to desire our best.

That is the difference between desire and expectation. Desire can be disappointed that someone missed out on what was best for them, but it is never angry because of it. Expectation on the other hand personalizes it as an offence against us and thus produces an angry response.

In order to solve this, all expectations in our lives should be limited to those God tells us we can have in the Bible. King David said in Psalm 62:5, "My soul, wait thou only upon God; for my expectation is from him." It is important to notice that David didn't say, my expectation is in God or on God, he said it is from God. In other words, if God said I can expect something then I can expect it, that is an expectation from God. When the Bible says in Romans 10:13, "For whosoever shall call upon the name of the Lord shall be saved." This means you can have a full expectation that if you call on Jesus Christ to forgive you, then you will be forgiven and saved from your sin. This is how you get an expectation from God. Some people put their false expectations on God by claiming that they expected God to keep them from having problems or to make things work out in their life. There is not a single verse in the Bible that obligates God to do that. As a matter of fact, the exact opposite is true, the Bible says that "Man is born unto trouble." The result of sin in this world guarantees that we will have problems and sorrow. God promises to forgive us if we turn to Him but even those who believe on Christ are not exempt from troubles while we are still in this world.

The one promise concerning our expectation that we can count on is that if we get our expectation from God we will be happy no matter what the circumstances around us. It says in Jeremiah 17:7-8, "Blessed is the man that trusteth in the LORD, and whose hope the LORD is. For he shall be as a tree planted by the waters, and that spreadeth out her roots by the river, and shall not see when heat cometh, but her leaf shall be green; and shall not be careful in the year of drought, neither shall cease from yielding fruit." The Word blessed in the Bible doesn't mean free of troubles, it means happy. When you have the right desires for others and limit your expectations only to what God has promised you will be happy because the Bible makes a great promise in Romans 8:28, "And we know that all things work together for good to them that love God, to them who are the called according to his purpose."

This specific situation may not be good, but if we leave it in God's hands He can take all things both good and bad and make them good in His time. I have seen very bad things happen to people and yet because they didn't respond in anger the end result was that very good things happened in their lives and the lives of others. Life isn't about what happens to you, it is about how you respond. You can keep those wrong expectations and live a life of personal disappointment and anger, destroying all the relationships in your life or you can put those wrong expectations away and live a life of peace and blessing.

Exercise: Answer the following questions.

Where do I get angry? Home / work / church / car / other:

_____

What expectation do I have in this place that I don't have in others?

_____

_____

Around who do I get angry the most?

_____

_____

_____

_____

What expectation do I have of them that I don't have of others?

_____

_____

What desire should I have <u>for</u> them instead of my unbiblical expectation <u>of</u> them?

_____

_____

Below on the left make a list of wrong expectations that you have in any area, then on the right make a list of what the right desire would be instead.

My wrong expectations   vs.   Right desires

_____   _____

_____   _____

_____   _____

_____   _____

_____   _____

_____   _____

Two

The Real Consequences of Anger

To understand the real consequences of anger you have to look no further than the 4th chapter of the Bible. We are going to start here and take a look at the downward progression that anger gives us and as we do we are going to elaborate on the far reaching effects that result. Begin with me in Genesis 4:3-5 "And in process of time it came to pass, that Cain brought of the fruit of the ground an offering unto the LORD. 4 And Abel, he also brought of the firstlings of his flock and of the fat thereof. And the LORD had respect unto Abel and to his offering: 5 But unto Cain and to his offering he had not respect. And Cain was very wroth, and his countenance fell."

Here we see the initial results of a broken expectation. Cain had a wrong expectation that God would accept his sacrifice no matter what. When God rejected Cain's sacrifice his expectation was broken and the result according to the scripture is that He became very wroth (angry) and his countenance fell. Isn't it amazing how when a person gives themselves over to anger you can see it in their countenance? The word countenance refers to the appearance of the face. You can see anger come over a person's face, that is exactly what the Bible is speaking of here with Cain. So, we have a broken expectation and a visible angry response. This is the beginning of anger, but it is not the end. God responds in verse 7 and says, "If thou doest well, shalt thou not be accepted? and if thou doest not well, sin lieth at the door. And unto thee shall be his desire, and thou shalt rule over him." He is speaking of our response here and is saying that your response is your decision. You can allow anger to have dominance in your life or you can reject it, but you will live with the results of that decision.

Cain chose to allow anger to continue in his heart. Ephesians 4:26-27 says, "Be ye angry, and sin not: let not the sun go down upon your wrath: 27 Neither give place to the devil." To allow anger to remain is sin according to the Bible. This verse by the way does not give license for anger, the tense of this phrase "be ye angry" is a passive tense, meaning to be provoked to anger but not to respond with anger. In other words, it could be said, be provoked but do not respond, don't allow anger to take hold in your heart. The reason is because when you do, you give place to the Devil. You allow a wrong spirit to control you. When a person is overcome by anger they respond in ways that are out of character for their normal personality. They are under the influence of anger and have given Satan a chance to work in them and in the situation. Cain did just this and the result of that is found in Genesis 4:8, "And Cain talked with Abel his brother: and it came to pass, when they were in the field, that Cain rose up against Abel his brother, and slew him."

When anger is not immediately rejected, and someone spends time entertaining it, it inevitably results in a someone taking the fall for our problem. If that person had not done what they did, then my situation would be different. This is called resentment. The inevitable result of resentment is bitterness, a vehement dislike and even hatred for another person. Here we see the result of that is vengeance. Cain took his anger, resentment and bitterness out on Able by killing him. Now you may say, my anger has never resulted in murder but this is exactly what Jesus implied was the end result of unleashed anger in Matthew 5:21-22, "Ye have heard that it was said by them of old time, Thou shalt not kill; and whosoever shall kill shall be in danger of the judgment: 22 But I say unto you, That whosoever is angry with his brother without a cause shall be in danger of the judgment: and whosoever shall say to his brother, Raca, shall be in danger of the council: but whosoever shall say, Thou fool, shall be in danger of hell fire." In God's eyes anger is equivalent to murder. No one commits murder who has not first given themselves to anger. Murder is the ultimate expression of anger and thus God says to start down the road of anger is to head toward the end result of murder. The statement here "angry without a cause" means that there is no cause to allow anger to continue. There is no justification before God to allow anger to have place in your life.

The next step in the downward progression of anger is in Genesis 4:9, "And the LORD said unto Cain, Where is Abel thy brother? And he said, I know not: Am I my brother's keeper?" When confronted with his actions Cain responded with denial. Of course, he knew where Abel was and yet he was not willing to acknowledge his error. Many people given to anger are also in great denial about it. I cannot tell you how many times I have counseled with families where it is obvious that anger is tearing the home apart and yet the angry person simply will not admit that they have a problem with anger. They feel justified in their anger. If everyone would just do what they are supposed to do, if people would just not bother them, and any number of other justifications are given. The sin of anger lends itself to justification so readily. Denial becomes a way of life, it is not my fault it is my wife's, my husbands, my children's, my parents, my boss's, other drivers, societies, we could go on and on but remember this, how you respond is always your decision. A sinful response to anger is always your fault.

What happens next in our text is telling because it is so often the case. God in response to Cain does not immediately judge him for murder, instead God passes a rather merciful judgment on him, but Cain will still not accept that this was his fault at all. He responds to God's mercy in verse 13 by saying, "And Cain said unto the LORD, My punishment is greater than I can bear." Ingratitude has now set into Cain's heart and though he has not received the judgment he deserves he is ungrateful. Angry people are often ungrateful for the kindnesses shown to them. They do not want justice they want vengeance. An angry person doesn't want things set right they want others destroyed. Therefore, they become increasingly ungrateful for any kindnesses shown to them.

The result of continued ingratitude is that a person begins to look at life from an increasingly negative and selfish way, only considering how everything is against them and how they have been mistreated and thus they become depressed. It says in verse 14, "Behold, thou hast driven me out this day from the face of the earth; and from thy face shall I be hid; and I shall be a fugitive and a vagabond in the earth; and it shall come to pass, that every one that findeth me shall slay me." Notice all the personal pronouns used here, "driven me out", "I be hid", "I shall be", "findeth me shall slay me". How dare you allow the same thing to happen to me that I have done to others. A total focus on self is one of the earmarks of depression. In many cases, it is the ultimate self-pity party. Finally, in verse 16 of our text is says, "And Cain went out from the presence of the LORD," Ultimately not dealing with anger properly results in leaving God completely and going off the deep end in life.

This downward progression illustrated:

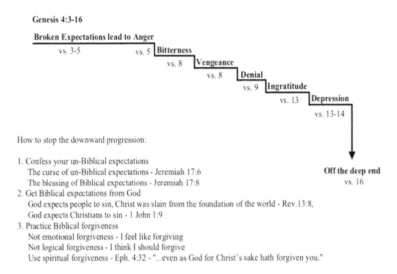

Genesis 4:3-16

Broken Expectations lead to Anger

vs. 3-5   vs. 5 **Bitterness**
                    vs. 8 **Vengeance**
                          vs. 8 **Denial**
                                vs. 9 **Ingratitude**
                                      vs. 13 **Depression**
                                              vs. 13-14

How to stop the downward progression:

1. Confess your un-Biblical expectations
   The curse of un-Biblical expectations - Jeremiah 17:6
   The blessing of Biblical expectations - Jeremiah 17:8
2. Get Biblical expectations from God
   God expects people to sin, Christ was slain from the foundation of the world - Rev.13:8,
   God expects Christians to sin - 1 John 1:9
3. Practice Biblical forgiveness
   Not emotional forgiveness - I feel like forgiving
   Not logical forgiveness - I think I should forgive
   Use spiritual forgiveness - Eph. 4:32 - "...even as God for Christ's sake hath forgiven you."

Off the deep end
vs. 16

Now that we have seen a specific example from the Bible of what anger produces, I want to elaborate on some detailed consequences of anger for a minute before we go on. Anger always produces strife and contention in a person's life. In the book of Proverbs, 3 times it talks about this. Proverbs 29:22, "An angry man stirreth up strife, and a furious man aboundeth in transgression." Again in, Proverbs 30:33 "Surely the churning of milk bringeth forth butter, and the wringing of the nose bringeth forth blood: so the forcing of wrath bringeth forth strife." And finally, in Proverbs 15:18 "A wrathful man stirreth up strife: but *he that is* slow to anger appeaseth strife." There is a constant when we deal with anger in people, those who are given to anger have lives that are filled with strife and contention. They inevitably have conflict in their homes and this destroys their marital relationships as well as their relationships with their children. Many children who grew up with an angry parent despise their parent for the constant strife that they endured at home. Yet they also unfortunately learn those angry responses. In reality, an angry person may be condemning their grandchildren to the same anger that they express in the home. Anger is so often a generational sin in families.

Anger produces a great burden that the individual must carry with them constantly. It says in Proverbs 27:3, "A stone *is* heavy, and the sand weighty; but a fool's wrath *is* heavier than them both." Imagine carrying a large stone around continually or a bag of sand, for a short distance it seems like it wouldn't matter but hold it very long and you will wear out quickly. Anger produces a great amount of stress in life. Doctors continually say that 60-80% of all illness is stress related. Holding onto anger is like carrying a weight of stress that is ultimately leading to your own death. It says as much in Job 5:2, "For wrath killeth the foolish man, and envy slayeth the silly one." Worse than killing yourself is the stress that you put on your family because you load them up with the stress of your anger. They never know when you might go off again. Your spouse and your children are continually walking on egg shells in their own home afraid that they will do something that will bring your ire is an incredible stress and has been known to cause many serious health and mental issues.

Finally, I want you to consider that anger, if not dealt with properly, will result in personal punishment. It says in Proverbs 19:19, "A man of great wrath shall suffer punishment: for if thou deliver *him*, yet thou must do it again." It may be losing your marriage, your children, your friends, your job, going to jail or some other consequence but you can mark this down for sure, there is a high cost to anger. We often say here, you can choose the sin, but you cannot choose the consequences. The cost is often much higher than you are willing to pay but you will have no choice of what it is.

Exercise:

Upon a prayerful examination, where are you in the downward progression illustrated here?

_____

What consequences have already taken place because of your anger?

_____

Make a list of those you need to forgive:

_____   _____

_____   _____

_____   _____

_____   _____

_____   _____

_____   _____

_____   _____

_____   _____

_____   _____

"The Lord is not slack concerning his promise, as some men count slackness; but is longsuffering to us-ward, not willing that any should perish, but that all should come to repentance."
~2 Peter 3:9

Three

What Must Be Done?

When anger has been an issue in your life and you have progressed downward as we saw in the last chapter the first thing that must be done is to practice Biblical forgiveness. The forgiveness that we extend will release us from the prison of emotion that we have bound ourselves in. Before we talk about how to forgive in a Biblical fashion, I want to discuss the dangers of not doing so. You may be tempted to simply ignore this step if you don't properly understand the danger you are in living with unforgiveness.

There are three spiritual consequences of allowing your anger to remain which have far reaching implications. The first consequence is that you have created a separation from God in your heart through the iniquity of unforgiveness. We are told in Isaiah 59:2 "But your iniquities have separated between you and your God, and your sins have hid his face from you, that he will not hear."

Iniquity in the Bible is expressed as a positive attitude toward unrighteousness or a negative attitude toward righteousness. It is not just what we do that affects our relationship with God, our heart attitude toward God and His Word affects our relationship as well. When we have a positive attitude toward the sin of anger or we willingly hold onto our resentment, bitterness, ingratitude, depression and so on, then we have created a separation with God.

The separation that is created by our unforgiveness results in our prayers not being heard. David expressed this as well in Psalm 66:18 "If I regard iniquity in my heart, the Lord will not hear me:" Think of how the fact of holding onto the iniquity of unforgiveness creates a situation that prevents your prayers from being heard by God. Often, I have heard that bitterness is a poison that we take hoping others will die but the reality is that when we allow this iniquity to remain we are actually killing our own relationship with God.

The extended implication of this is that when we refuse to forgive we also eliminate ourselves from the forgiveness of God. We will address this more later but the grace of God to cover our own transgression is removed because of this, and now we are faced with the devastating effect of bitterness due to the lack of God's grace for living being present in our lives.

The second consequence is that you have given Satan a place in your life to hinder you. Remember what Paul told us about the relationship of the Devil to anger in Ephesians 4:26-27 "Be ye angry, and sin not: let not the sun go down upon your wrath: Neither give place to the devil." When we don't practice forgiveness, and remove anger we give the devil a place of residence in our lives.

This thought is extended on in 2 Corinthians 2:10-11 "To whom ye forgive any thing, I forgive also: for if I forgave any thing, to whom I forgave it, for your sakes forgave I it in the person of Christ; Lest Satan should get an advantage of us: for we are not ignorant of his devices." The device of Satan to hinder us is employed by the effecting of our thinking. As a matter of fact, this is often what we mean when we refer to strong holds. The issue of strong holds is discussed in great detail in the following verses.

2 Corinthians 10:3-6 "For though we walk in the flesh, we do not war after the flesh: (For the weapons of our warfare are not carnal, but mighty through God to the pulling down of strong holds;) Casting down imaginations, and every high thing that exalteth itself against the knowledge of God, and bringing into captivity every thought to the obedience of Christ; And having in a readiness to revenge all disobedience, when your obedience is fulfilled."

I see in this passage three C's that must be dealt with in order to have victory over a strong hold of the mind. The first is that we must cast down the sinful imaginations. Imaginations are the seeds of our thoughts, they might be described as the temptation to sinful thinking. This might be the initial thoughts of anger that enter your mind. The temptation to allow anger to take hold is strengthened by giving into that temptation in the past. Satan knows that he has a strong hold in your mind concerning anger and the introduction of offences or the bolstering of expectations only serves to keep you bound in the same fashion. These thoughts must be cast down, we must reject them with extreme prejudice because they have allowed our advisory to have an advantage over us in life.

The second "C" is to capture the thought. We will discuss using a trigger list to do this in a later chapter. Far too often we fail to identify exactly what is provoking our anger, we look at the people present and blame them rather than examining the thinking process that brought up the emotion within us. To capture the thought means to examine it. Ask yourself the questions, why did I get angry? What expectation did I have here? What other factors could be contributing to my emotional state?

The third "C" is to correct the thought. This is where we reject the anger and choose to forgive. If we don't do this then we are allowing the Devil to have the strong hold in our lives that will keep us bound and bring destruction into our lives. To illustrate the process we just talked about take a minute to examine the diagram at the end of this chapter.

The third consequence is that you have allowed yourself to be turned over to the tormentors. This issue is discussed by Jesus in the following passage.

Mat 18:21-35 "Then came Peter to him, and said, Lord, how oft shall my brother sin against me, and I forgive him? till seven times? Jesus saith unto him, I say not unto thee, Until seven times: but, Until seventy times seven. Therefore is the kingdom of heaven likened unto a certain king, which would take account of his servants. And when he had begun to reckon, one was brought unto him, which owed him ten thousand talents. But forasmuch as he had not to pay, his lord commanded him to be sold, and his wife, and children, and all that he had, and payment to be made. The servant therefore fell down, and worshipped him, saying, Lord, have patience with me, and I will pay thee all. Then the lord of that servant was moved with compassion, and loosed him, and forgave him the debt. But the same servant went out, and found one of his fellowservants, which owed him an hundred pence: and he laid hands on him, and took him by the throat, saying, Pay me that thou owest. And his fellowservant fell down at his feet, and besought him, saying, Have patience with me, and I will pay thee all. And he would not: but went and cast him into prison, till he should pay the debt. So when his fellowservants saw what was done, they were very sorry, and came and told unto their lord all that was done. Then his lord, after that he had called him, said unto him, O thou wicked servant, I forgave thee all that debt, because thou desiredst me: Shouldest not thou also have had compassion on thy fellowservant, even as I had pity on thee? And his lord was wroth, and delivered him to the tormentors, till he should pay all that was due unto him. So likewise shall my heavenly Father do also unto you, if ye from your hearts forgive not every one his brother their trespasses."

Obviously, the context of the passage here is the issue of forgiveness. Without going into a full discussion of this text I want to focus us in on the last few verses. It is told to us by Christ that the unforgiving servant was cast into prison and turned over to the tormentors because of his wicked spirit. The most astounding statement is made following this revelation in verse 35 though, "So likewise shall my heavenly Father do also unto you, if ye from your hearts forgive not every one his brother their trespasses."

Jesus says here that if we do not forgive we will also be turned over to the tormentors by our heavenly Father. The term tormentors is defined in the Webster's 1828 dictionary as: "He or that which torments; one who inflicts penal anguish or tortures." Jesus then is saying that when we won't forgive others we are turned over to those who will inflict torment upon us, that is the same as saying that we are turned over to be tormented by the devils.

The word torment is defined in the Webster's 1828 as "Extreme pain; anguish; the utmost degree of misery, either of body or mind.

or That which gives pain, vexation or misery." I believe that many are tormented by fear, anxiety, paranoia, regret and many other emotional conditions because they have refused to forgive someone. The list of what are called psychological conditions that could be a result of this is staggering. To think that something as simple as forgiveness could be the answer to what has people committed to mental hospitals is amazing. To think that many are on drug therapy for years because they simply refuse to forgive is sad and troubling but it is a reality none the less.

It could be that the issues that you are struggling with in other areas of your life are the direct result of allowing yourself to be bound because of unforgiveness. This doesn't have to be the case, in the next chapter we will examine how real forgiveness works.

3 C's
Dealing with Temptation
2 Corinthians 10:3-6

Imaginations	2 Corinthians 10:5 →	Thoughts	Hebrews 4:12 →	Intents
(The spark of thought)		(To consider in the mind)		(The determination to act)

1. Cast Down Imaginations

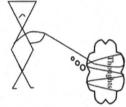

You don't have to allow your imagination to control what you think about. You can take control of your thinking by casting down any imaginations that are against God. To do this, you must be watchful against lustful thoughts as they come into your mind and cast them down as soon as they come in. Don't allow those imaginations to linger into thought. Mark 14:38; 1 Corinthians 16:13; 1 Thessalonians 5:6

2. Capture Thoughts

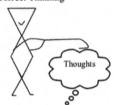

Once you have cast down sinful imaginations, bring your thoughts captive by determining where the sinful imagination came from. To do this we make a trigger list. A trigger list is just a small note pad that we write down the times when a sinful imagination comes in. We then ask, "Was there something that caused me to have that imagination?" If we determine that there was a trigger, we cut the cords that were holding that there by fasting. Proverbs 5:22; Isaiah 58:3-12

3. Correct Thinking

Correcting your thinking is what the Bible calls "bringing into obedience." You can do this by doing a stroke file, quoting Scripture, singing hymns, or simply putting your thoughts on the things listed in Philippians 4:8. You decide what things you are going to think on rather than allowing the world, the flesh, and the devil to have control of your thoughts.

"The Lord is not slack concerning his promise, as some men count slackness; but is longsuffering to us-ward, not willing that any should perish, but that all should come to repentance."
~2 Peter 3:9

Four

How Forgiveness Works

We are at the point now that we need to break down the mechanics of spiritual forgiveness that follows God's personal example.

> "And be ye kind one to another, tenderhearted, forgiving one another, even as God for Christ's sake hath forgiven you." Ephesians 4:32

We first want to focus in on how God forgives so that we can have a proper reference for how we are to forgive. To illustrate this, consider the following diagram.

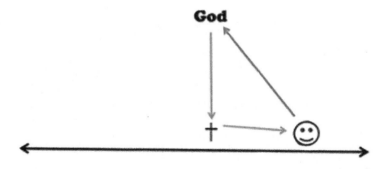

In this diagram, we see the line at the bottom as a representation of all time, the arrows represent that God's plan was formed before our beginning and continues after this world ends. God, of course, set at the top supersedes time. God is not bound by time; it is a constraint only for us. The Bible tells us that God set His plan for our atonement in motion before the creation of this world in 1 Peter 1:18-20, "Forasmuch as ye know that ye were not redeemed with corruptible things, as silver and gold, from your vain conversation received by tradition from your fathers; But with the precious blood of Christ, as of a lamb without blemish and without spot: Who verily was foreordained before the foundation of the world, but was manifest in these last times for you,"

Our diagram shows Christ's sacrifice for us represented by the cross. Around 2,000 years later, you and I came on the scene. The decision to forgive sin and the just method for forgiveness had already been determined and made. God's plan was already established before you were born and before you committed your first sin. As a matter of fact, God decided that He would forgive you before you asked Him to. His decision for forgiveness was not dependent upon your repentance; He was not waiting to see if you would repent before He chose to accept Christ's payment as sufficient to cover your sins. When you came to God and asked for forgiveness, He didn't have to think about it, He didn't have to examine all your sins and decide if Christ's payment was sufficient. He had already decided that the atonement was sufficient. The separation between you and God was not His willingness to forgive but your lack of repentance.

Please understand, the choice of forgiveness on God's part is distinct from our restoration to Him. We are told in 2 Peter 3:9, "The Lord is not slack concerning his promise, as some men count slackness; but is longsuffering to us-ward, not willing that any should perish, but that all should come to repentance." God made sufficient atonement for everyone and desires that all would receive His forgiveness by repentance, but He will not violate our free will to make us do so. God's heart of love toward us is expressed in His offer of restoration based upon His atonement for our forgiveness. This love will not violate His righteous judgment though, and as a result, whoever rejects His forgiveness will forever be separated by eternal death and suffer the wrath of God against sin that it rightly deserves. God is not unrighteous in this because He is not only willing to forgive but also Himself made the atonement necessary for our reconciliation.

You see, forgiveness is one side of the coin of restoration; the other side is repentance. When our repentance meets God's forgiveness, we find a restoration of our relationship with Him. Often those who hurt us will try to use the idea of forgiveness and our faith against us by demanding that if we were a real Christian, we would just forgive them. By this, they mean that we would accept them in their sin and do whatever they want. This is a perverted idea of forgiveness. God's love has extended forgiveness to us, but restoration is a different matter. God does not restore a relationship with us until we have acknowledged our wrongdoing and turned to Him; this is what the Bible calls repentance.

God does not accept our sin. He is able to do what most men cannot: He separates us from our sin. God judges our sin and forgives us upon our salvation. The devil loves to try to tie our identity to our sinful actions. The Devil would have you to believe that you are what you have done in your past, but God sees you as what He created you to be rather than what you have done in your sin. It is important to remember that you are not what you have done, but what you are you will do. When you are a lost sinner, you will do the works of the flesh. When you are made a new creature in Christ Jesus, the inner man which is created after righteousness desires to do the things of the Spirit of God.

Forgiveness is a choice on God's part not to carry the burden of our sin forever upon Himself, but rather to choose the sacrifice of Christ as sufficient, and thus, the burden is alleviated. For God, forgiveness is a fixed point. The entire Old Testament pointed toward the Messiah that would come, and the entire New Testament points at the Messiah who did. From the point of His death, burial, and resurrection, there is nothing left to carry of sin; it has all been judged at that fixed point.

Forgiveness on God's part is also transactional. We come to God with our burden of sin and He exchanges it for the righteousness of Christ. All that filthiness was already judged, and an abundant source of righteousness is now available to all who call upon the LORD.

God does not examine us to see if we deserve forgiveness, to see if we will offend again, or to see if we have done enough to earn it. God looks at Christ and says that He was sufficient, and in this manner, God for Christ's sake forgives us. If you are saved, it is not because of you; it is because you came to God in repentance and God for Christ's sake forgave you. As we are reminded in Ephesians 2:8-9, "For by grace are ye saved through faith; and that not of yourselves: it is the gift of God: Not of works, lest any man should boast." How could you boast of your forgiveness from God when it was not about you?

Now consider the next aspect of forgiveness, namely how we extend it to others.

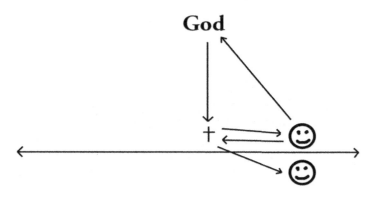

Ephesians 4:32 told us that we are to be "forgiving one another even as God for Christ's sake hath forgiven you". Now that you understand how God for Christ's sake has forgiven you, you can apply that to your situation. When someone has hurt you, you have the choice to carry that with you by being angry, bitter, full of wrath, malice, and so on, or you can follow God's example and take that offense to the cross. It isn't about examining the individual; you should not do that anymore than God has done it with you. Remember that in the Old Testament when someone brought their sacrifice to the temple, the priest examined the sacrifice to see if it was sufficient; he didn't examine the one who brought it.

The only question that matters when you are considering the issue of forgiving someone else is, was Christ's atonement sufficient to cover that offense? The answer is always yes! Since Christ's atonement covers the offense, we can forgive just as God has. We go to the fixed point of the cross and conduct a transaction where we give God the offense and we take the righteousness of Christ to cover it. I can forgive you for Christ's sake because that is how I have been forgiven.

Some people struggle with the idea of forgiving those who have hurt them for a couple reasons. Maybe you have thought that forgiving would mean that you are saying what they did was okay. Of course, it wasn't okay. God never said our sin was okay; He said it was sufficiently paid for by the sacrifice of Christ. Maybe you have been resistant to forgiving because you have thought that if you did, you were saying that they could hurt you again. Remember, however, that forgiveness is not the same thing as restoration. Forgiveness is taking the burden of their offense off of you and placing it where God did: on Christ. Forgiveness is about your heart more than it is about theirs. Even God could not keep all the offenses of men and forgive at the same time. He had to judge the offenses which gave Him the freedom to forgive us. He has done the same for you. If you count the offenses as judged in Christ, then you can lay them aside regardless of what the offender does.

This is not only what Paul tells us to do in Ephesians, but it is what he practiced. In 2 Corinthians, Paul is discussing the forgiveness of someone who had been disciplined out of the church and how to restore them back. The individual in question had repented of their wrongdoing and desired to be restored back to the church. He says,

> "To whom ye forgive any thing, I forgive also: for
> if I forgave any thing, to whom I forgave it, for
> your sakes forgave I it in the person of Christ; Lest
> Satan should get an advantage of us: for we are not
> ignorant of his devices."
> 2 Corinthians 2:10-11

Notice that Paul practiced what he preached: Anyone he forgave was forgiven in the person of Christ. That is exactly what we are talking about here. Paul took the offense to Christ and judged that the payment was made, so he exchanged the offense for Christ's payment and was able to forgive.

Jesus discussed the issue of forgiveness and the lack of it when giving the disciples the model prayer.

> "And forgive us our debts, as we forgive our debtors." Matthew 6:12

> "For if ye forgive men their trespasses, your heavenly Father will also forgive you: But if ye forgive not men their trespasses, neither will your Father forgive your trespasses."
> Matthew 6:14-15

First, Christ teaches them to pray for personal forgiveness and then to extend that forgiveness to others. It is likely that if you recognize your own need for forgiveness, then you will be more willing to forgive others. Jesus then goes on to tie our forgiveness of others to our own forgiveness from God. This may seem somewhat strange until you consider His atonement. You see, we have already shown that the penalty for sin was set as a universal standard that applied to all men and that the payment for sin was set the same way. Consider, then, that if the payment was intended by God to be sufficient for all, that means that when I despise the forgiveness of God for someone else, I am despising it for myself as well. How could I say that God's forgiveness is sufficient to cover my sins but not great enough to cover theirs? I have, at that point, limited the sufficiency of Christ's atonement, and if I do that, it is no longer the atonement that God accepted; I have perverted it in order to retain my offense. This makes such a sacrifice part of another gospel, but God doesn't accept alternate gospels. I must accept it as God intended it or not accept it at all. God's forgiveness is sufficient to cover all sin, but my perversion of it cannot even cover my own. We would be much better off to use God's standard and reject the idea that we know better than Him.

Exercise: Using the list of those that you need to forgive that you made in the last chapter take each of these people and their offenses to God one by one. Acknowledge that they have hurt you but also your belief that Christ's payment was sufficient to cover their sin, then choose to forgive based upon Christ's atonement. Once you have forgiven, cross the offense off your paper.

"Looking diligently lest any man fail of
the grace of God; lest any root of
bitterness springing up trouble you, and
thereby many be defiled;"
~Hebrews 12:15

Five

A Final Warning About Bitterness

This chapter originally appeared in the book "Life's Toolbox"

Several years ago, after being in the ministry for just a short time, I had a foolish conflict with another pastor. The cause of this conflict is unimportant, but the result of this conflict would plague me for most of a year. Finally, God brought me to a place of seeing just how much damage I was doing to myself, both emotionally and spiritually. I praise the Lord that through His word, I was able to forsake the bitterness that had poisoned my soul. This event caused me to look at bitterness in a new way than I had before. As we explore bitterness for the next few minutes I will use my own example of struggle to try and bring forth some spiritual truths that will help others caught in this battle to free themselves from the poison of bitterness.

Hebrews 12:15 "Looking diligently lest any man fail of the grace of God; lest any root of bitterness springing up trouble you, and thereby many be defiled;" *I* grew up in church and in a good Christian home. Many times I have heard this verse alluded to and preached in one form or another. Yet I failed to make the connection given in this verse to the source of bitterness in our lives. As you look at this verse, you see the opening warning, "Looking diligently lest any man fail of the grace of God;". Considering this statement, it is without any reservation that I say that the grace of God has never failed, and will never fail. That is not the basis of this statement. The point of the statement is that you and I can fail of the grace of God. We can fail to possess an adequate amount of God's grace to face the trials of life. Please understand this does not have anything to do with salvation. There are two aspects that we will perceive of the grace of God. First, His saving grace. God's grace is able to save all those who call upon Him without fail, yes, His grace was, is, and forever will be able to forgive all sin. The other aspect of His grace that is significant is His grace for living. That is to say, the grace that He gives His children to live in this evil world. It is of that latter grace that we are in danger of falling short. James gives an indication of how this happens when he says in James 4:6, "But he giveth more grace. Wherefore he saith, God resisteth the proud, but giveth grace unto the humble." You see two groups here, the humble, to whom God is bestowing grace, and the proud, whom He is resisting. I think it safe to say that if God is able to bestow more grace upon the humble, than that implies that He in similar fashion resists the proud by withdrawing His grace. Again, not saving grace, but grace for living. In effect, He says, OK, you think that you are really something, you think that you can handle it on your own. Well, let's see how you do without my grace to guide you through. God withdraws His grace in from our lives in areas of pride. Now remember the warning of Hebrews, "lest any man fail of the grace of God". When we become lifted up in pride, God withdraws His grace for living from our lives. Then when an injustice comes into our lives (it may be real or perceived), with the grace of God removed, we fall into bitterness. We are troubled and are in danger of defiling others.

Let's take a few moments and look at Jonah who I believe was a prime example of the effects of bitterness in the life of a child of God. By chapter four of Jonah, Nineveh has repented, God has forgiven them, and Jonah has rebelled again. Jonah 4:1-3 says, "But it displeased Jonah exceedingly, and he was very angry. And he prayed unto the LORD, and said, I pray thee, O LORD, was not this my saying, when I was yet in my country? Therefore I fled before unto Tarshish: for I knew that thou art a gracious God, and merciful, slow to anger, and of great kindness, and repentest thee of the evil. Therefore now, O LORD, take, I beseech thee, my life from me; for it is better for me to die than to live." Here we find the first of five consequences to bitterness in the life of Jonah. The first consequence is that bitterness causes you to despise the forgiveness of God. Jonah couldn't believe that God would forgive the Ninevites. Some Bible doubters wondered if Nineveh even existed. Then in the 1800s, British adventurer Austen Henry Layard rediscovered the lost palace and city across the Tigris River from modern day Mosul in northern Iraq.

Jonah lived during the height of the Assyrian empire. Based on the tablets excavated in Nineveh, the Assyrians were very brutal, ruthless people. They frequently raided the Northern kingdom where Jonah lived, destroying many villages and towns. The Jews hated the Ninevites. Imagine Jonah's horror when God asked him to take a message to these enemies of goodness. I can't help but picture in my mind this whole city repenting, and Jonah stomping his feet and yelling at God, "I knew this would happen! I knew that if they heard this message they would all repent and you would forgive them! That's why I didn't want to come in the first place!" Imagine the worst civilization today, and one preacher showing up in the heart of their most wicked city with the message of repent or God is going to destroy you. Would you have so much faith in that message that you would say the same thing as Jonah? We criticize Jonah, yet this was a man who believed God. This also was a man who was proud to be part of God's chosen people. The Jews looked down upon the Assyrian "dogs"; they were better than these uncivilized heathens. Why would God ask Jonah to take a message of repentance to people who obviously deserved to die? Why not just kill them and be done with it? Oh, how great is the mercy of our God. Yet in his bitter state, Jonah despised the forgiveness that God was giving to Nineveh.

When I experienced the perceived injustice in my life I began to pray for God to judge the individual that had "wronged" me. I hope that you are more spiritual than I was, but I went so far as to suggest to God what He could do to punish the offender. I look back on this with shame; I was almost like David in his imprecatory Psalms, though operating in the flesh. I did not want God to forgive the offender; I wanted justice for myself. I was proud and wanted God to reinforce that I was right. The biggest problem with this is that when you despise God's forgiveness for someone else, you mar your own forgiveness from God. Matthew 6:15 says, "But if ye forgive not men their trespasses, neither will your Father forgive your trespasses." I place myself under the judgment of God, which means that I have no right to bring my petitions to the throne of God. Psalm 66:18 says, "If I regard iniquity in my heart, the Lord will not hear me". You need to understand that when you are in bitterness, you have cut off your line of communication with God.

It is also important to know that God says in Romans 13 that vengeance belongs to Him alone. As long as you stand in front of the offender ordering God to judge them, God most likely will not. You hinder God from dealing with them because of your own pride. What a shame that our insistence on being right can hinder the work of God and bring sin into our own life.

The second consequence of bitterness is found in verses 4-5 of Jonah chapter number four: "Then said the LORD, Doest thou well to be angry? So Jonah went out of the city, and sat on the east side of the city, and there made him a booth, and sat under it in the shadow, till he might see what would become of the city." This consequence is that bitterness causes you to develop a singular focus on your enemy to the neglect of your own need. Imagine the city of Nineveh has repented and God has accepted, but Jonah, filled with his own sense of justice, goes out of the city, sits on the side of a hill and says, "I am going to sit here until God comes to his senses and kills these people!" I imagine that God may have had more things for Jonah to do, yet he was so focused on his enemy that he could not see anything else. Bitterness causes you to be spiritually blind. I remember during those dark days of my life, asking people who knew this other person, how that other person was doing, but only to find out if God had started the judgment yet. I inwardly longed to hear bad things were happening to them. It is amazing as I have met and dealt with others that are in the gall of bitterness just how singularly focused they are. Their whole life seems to pivot on a singular event or relationship. Often the other party is oblivious to this and lives a normal life, while these pine away in sorrow. Someone once said that bitterness is a pill you swallow hoping someone else will die. Yet, it is you who will suffer, ignoring all the good things of your life, laboring under the false pretense that if God did judge them that it would somehow vindicate you and make you feel better. You have succumbed to a lie.

The third consequence of bitterness is found in the next couple of verses. Jonah 4:6-8 "And the LORD God prepared a gourd, and made it to come up over Jonah, that it might be a shadow over his head, to deliver him from his grief. So Jonah was exceeding glad of the gourd. But God prepared a worm when the morning rose the next day, and it smote the gourd that it withered. And it came to pass, when the sun did arise, that God prepared a vehement east wind; and the sun beat upon the head of Jonah, that he fainted, and wished in himself to die, and said, It is better for me to die than to live." This consequence is evident to everyone but the infected: pettiness. I have yet to meet a bitter person that isn't petty. I have been in church my whole life, but I have only seen one church split that was over doctrine. I was recently told that doctrine divides but in churches it is usually the color of the carpet, the decorations in the bathroom, the plants in the entryway... the list goes on and on and it all boils down to one thing, pettiness. Every preacher could give you a number of examples of the petty things people have done to others in the church because of bitterness.

Bitter people do things out of spite. Here sits Jonah, the recipient of God's mercy, both spiritually and now physically. He is sheltered in his bitterness by a gourd. How thankful he is for the gourd. And yet as God shows a picture of what bitterness really is to Jonah, a worm that eats at your insides until you die, he gets angry at God again. Bitter people frequently get angry at those who try to help them out of the pit they are in. I am justified to feel this way, they say. If you would have suffered what I did you would feel the same way. Can you hear Jonah crying for the gourd, that petty little thing that was given to help him see his folly? It was unsettling to God to hear him cry over a gourd and at the same time wish death upon hundreds of thousands of people. My own pettiness was manifest in the fact that I decided to warn the object of my bitterness in a letter of the impending doom of God upon him. After God showed me my wickedness, I couldn't believe that I would do such a wicked thing. If you and I received the just reward for our sins, God would strike us down right this minute. Yet we have a compassionate, longsuffering God. He was with me, in bringing me through His word to a place of forgiveness.

The fourth consequence is somewhat prophesied in Proverbs 13:12 "Hope deferred maketh the heart sick: but when the desire cometh, it is a tree of life." While the judgment of those you are bitter against will not bring a tree of life into your heart, the deferred hope of their judgment will make your heart sick, and you will eventually sink into depression just as Jonah did in Jonah 4:9, "And God said to Jonah, Doest thou well to be angry for the gourd? And he said, I do well to be angry, even unto death." Maybe you have thought the same thing concerning your bitterness: I do well to be angry until I die. Depression is rarely an organic physical problem or one that is unrelated to emotional issues. It is caused most often by sin. Here Jonah looks in the face of God and says in effect I will not get right. Be careful, there is a line you can cross with God. 1 John 5:16, "If any man see his brother sin a sin which is not unto death, he shall ask, and he shall give him life for them that sin not unto death. There is a sin unto death: I do not say that he shall pray for it." When you come to the place that you tell God you will not get right you are in danger of crossing a deadline with God. God is very longsuffering and gives us many opportunities to turn but there is a point in which He stops you from harming others. I praise God that He pulled me out of this mess before I came to this point, but I have met many who did not get right. They fell into depression; the world told them it was because they didn't like themselves enough. The truth is that many times it is the opposite: they liked themselves too much. They are many times prideful and do not believe that they deserve the treatment that they are receiving from others and God, thus they fall into depression. You can still be salvaged even if you have gotten this far. It is not yet too late for you to be restored to the truth. The answer is not drugs though, the answer is the Bible. In just a few minutes we will address a specific answer for you.

The last consequence is unstated, yet I believe is implied and born out by historical facts. Jonah 4:10-11 says, "Then said the LORD, Thou hast had pity on the gourd, for the which thou hast not laboured, neither madest it grow; which came up in a night, and perished in a night: And should not I spare Nineveh, that great city, wherein are more than sixscore thousand persons that cannot discern between their right hand and their left hand; and also much cattle?" Just a little distance from Nineveh is a mosque that claims to be the burial place of Jonah. The scripture is devoid of a further mention of the life of Jonah. The last time we see him is sitting on the side of the hill in bitterness asking God to kill him for the third time. I believe the last consequence of bitterness is death. First spiritual, then physical. The fact that you are reading this is a sign that you still have a chance to get things right, to avoid this final consequence. But how? The answer to that is found where we started just a few pages back.

If the Bible is right, the source of bitterness is a failure of the grace of God, and that failure is caused by God's grace being withdrawn from the proud. It only stands to reason that you must humble yourself to receive the grace of God to cover this sin. James 4:7-9 gives a three-step process to humbling one's self. "Submit yourselves therefore to God. Resist the devil, and he will flee from you. Draw nigh to God, and he will draw nigh to you. Cleanse your hands, ye sinners; and purify your hearts, ye double minded. Be afflicted, and mourn, and weep: let your laughter be turned to mourning, and your joy to heaviness." The first step in the process of humbling yourself is to submit to God your thinking and feelings. Surrender your right to feel anger and bitterness. Admit that your thinking has not solved the problem. Your thinking and feelings have magnified the problem and must be surrendered to His thinking and feelings. 2 Corinthians 2:10-11 says, "To whom ye forgive any thing, I forgive also: for if I forgave any thing, to whom I forgave it, for your sakes forgave I it in the person of Christ; Lest Satan should get an advantage of us: for we are not ignorant of his devices." Paul implies here that the only way to forgive anyone is to do so through yielding your thinking and feelings to Christ. You may have tried to forgive the person in the past; it could be that you even have punished yourself for not being a good enough Christian to stop feeling and thinking the way you do about them. The answer is that you cannot do it through your own power. As Paul looked on those who had wronged him (and they were many) he pictured Jesus on the cross. As He was on the cross, He was looking down through time and saw every sin that would be committed, and His choice on the cross was to forgive each and every one of them, even the ones that would be committed against you. Paul chose to stop going by his own thinking and feelings and make a conscience choice to go by Christ's. Forgiveness is a choice, not a feeling. This choice begins with the first step of humbling yourself and submitting your thinking and feelings to God. Submit your wounded heart and spirit, and it will amaze you how quickly He can heal it.

The second step in this humbling process is that of resisting the Devil and drawing nigh to God. The act of resisting is summed up in the act of drawing nigh. You cannot resist the Devil by your own power, but as you draw nigh to God, the Devil must flee. One of my favorite illustrations of the Father's response to us is the prodigal son. I have heard it said it is just as far back to the house as it was when you left. This may be true, but it is not as far back to the Father. The Bible tells us that the Father was watching and when he saw His son a great way off He ran to meet him. James reinforces this thought when he says draw nigh to God, and He will draw nigh to you. Every step you take toward God is equal to two. The blessed thing about the story is that the son was in the Fathers embrace long before he reached the house; it was the Father that ultimately brought the son back to the house.

The Bible tells us that the Devil is limited in where he can go, and what he can do by the Father. The Devil must keep a certain distance from God, as you draw nigh to Him, the Devil must flee. How do you draw nigh to God? The answer is basic: through prayer, Bible reading, and church attendance. You may say you have been doing those things and it hasn't worked. No, you have been doing those things while filled with pride and being resisted by the Father. You may have been doing the right things, but with the wrong spirit, God was pushing you away. Once you come in a humbled spirit, you will find the Father responds differently to you. Look at these verses: Psalm 34:18 "The LORD is nigh unto them that are of a broken heart; and saveth such as be of a contrite spirit." Psalm 51:17 "The sacrifices of God are a broken spirit: a broken and a contrite heart, O God, thou wilt not despise." Isaiah 57:15 "For thus saith the high and lofty One that inhabiteth eternity, whose name is Holy; I dwell in the high and holy place, with him also that is of a contrite and humble spirit, to revive the spirit of the humble, and to revive the heart of the contrite ones." Humility is precious in the sight of God, He wants to receive you but you must come on His terms.

The third step in humbling yourself is what is listed in the last of James 4:8-9 "Cleanse your hands, ye sinners; and purify your hearts, ye double minded. Be afflicted, and mourn, and weep: let your laughter be turned to mourning, and your joy to heaviness." To humble yourself and receive the grace of God back on your life, you must confess that you have been in sin. God is not as concerned with the offence as your response to it. You have sinned; you have been in unforgiveness and bitterness. It must be confessed for what it is: SIN. We have a tendency to justify and rename sin to make it sound more acceptable, but God will have none of it. If you want healing, you must call it what God does, and you must be sorry for it. Not sorry for what it has done to you, but sorry for what you have done to a just, holy, and righteous God.

Let's take a minute to address those who have possibly slipped as far into bitterness as depression. The Bible answer for you is to begin to look for things to praise God for. Start by setting your expectations in God instead of man as David said in Psalm 62:5, "My soul, wait thou only upon God; for my expectation is from him." Then, apply Isaiah 61:3 "To appoint unto them that mourn in Zion, to give unto them beauty for ashes, the oil of joy for mourning, the garment of praise for the spirit of heaviness; that they might be called trees of righteousness, the planting of the LORD, that he might be glorified." Praise to God raises the spirit of man. Begin to make lists of things that you can see and think of to praise God for. Do so audibly, the Devil does not like to hear the praises of God, but the habit of praising God with your mouth will draw you up out of depression.

Back to James, I love verse ten of James 4 which says, "Humble yourselves in the sight of the Lord, and he shall lift you up." He will lift you up out of pride, bitterness, depression, you name it, He will lift you up when you follow the Biblical recipe for humility.

One last thing that I wish to address is what happened to me when I finally gave the issue of my bitterness over to God. Suddenly it dawned on me how sinful I had been, I remembered the prayers and wishes for God to judge the other individual. I was crushed by this. I began to beg God to forgive them as well, not to judge them. My heart became heavy, I sought their forgiveness for holding bitterness against them. To this day, I pray for them frequently, that God would bless them. When your heart is right, you will not desire the judgment of God upon others; you will desire them to receive the same mercy that you received undeservingly. What joy it is to pray for God to bless others rather than curse them. This must have been how the author felt when he wrote in Psalm 133:1 "Behold, how good and how pleasant it is for brethren to dwell together in unity!" Please, I ask you to heed the warning of the Scriptures as to the destructive nature of bitterness! If you are ensnared by it, follow these Biblical steps to overcome this trap of the Devil. You are not ignorant of his devises. Peace and joy await you when you humble yourself.

"Be not hasty in thy spirit to be angry: for anger resteth in the bosom of fools."
~Ecclesiastes 7:9

Six

Steps to Overcoming Anger

Decide to stop anger – Psalm 37:8 "Cease from anger, and forsake wrath: fret not thyself in any wise to do evil." Step 1 may sound over simplistic but let me be clear, you will never make any headway on dealing with anger until you make the decision that you are going to eliminate it in your life. You do not need to just get better control of it, that is like having control of a wild beast, it may seem in control but if it ever gets out it will destroy. You need to eliminate it from your life and you must make the decision that you are going to do just that. Until you make a full commitment to dealing with anger you will continue to struggle with it.

Let me give you my personal testimony here. I had a terrible anger problem. I was constantly fighting with my wife, I would yell and scream, at times I got so angry I would punch the wall. I stomped my feet and even threw things, never at my wife, but I believe that was just a progression away from where I was headed. I knew that my anger was a major problem, but I didn't know what to do about it. One night in church God got hold of my heart about my anger issue. I don't remember what the preacher was talking about, I do not believe it had anything to do with anger to be honest with you, but that is what God was dealing with me about. For the first time in my life I realized that I must deal with my anger or it was going to cost me my family. I went to the alter that service and confessed to

God that I had an anger problem and I turned myself over to Him in that area. I made a commitment to God that I would not allow anger to have dominance over me any longer and that I would dedicate myself to learning how to deal with problems from a Biblical prospective rather than trying to solve problems in my anger.

The reality is that anger is deceptive because it does seem to aid in solving problems, but it doesn't actually accomplish what it seems to. If people stop an action out of fear they have not had a change of heart about the issue and thus we are going to have continued problems and now we have compounded them by anger. I went home, and I told my wife that I had made a commitment to God to get rid of anger in my life and I would not be fighting with her any more. I want you to know that my decision to remove anger and not fight any longer was sincere but that does not mean it wasn't tested. I had allowed anger to become the normal way of dealing with conflict in my home and my wife had not made the same commitment that I had. It took time to show her that I was serious about not resorting to anger to solve problems. I will deal with that issue more fully when we talk about restoring relationships damaged by anger. Suffice it so say for now, that you must make this decision and commit yourself to God in it.

Eliminate wrong expectations – Psalm 62:5 "My soul, wait thou only upon God; for my expectation is from him." Our first chapter dealt with the problem of wrong expectations in a detailed fashion, I am not going to rehash all the issues here but if you are going to deal with anger you must evaluate your expectations. When you get angry you must ask the question what expectation did I have and is it in line with God's plan for expectations. As I said before it is ok to have a desire, to desire someone to do right is ok, but to expect them to do right is not ok. Desire is for their best, they are at their best when they do what they should, but expectation puts them under a burden to perform and makes us the one holding the weight of their performance. Remember, everyone in this world including you is only human, everyone fails, everyone messes up including you. The golden rule is so applicable here, do unto others as you would have them do unto you. Despite what you might think you are not perfect; your way is not the only way and you must treat others with the same respect that you desire when you fail.

As soon as you get angry you need to ask yourself the question, "what expectation did I have? This reminds you that the problem was you having unbiblical expectations. At that point you must repent of that expectation and restructure your thinking. The Bible calls this renewing the mind, changing the way that you think about something. We will address in the next point a specific strategy to do that.

Don't be hasty – this is mentioned 3 times in the Bible, it says in Ecclesiastes 7:9 "Be not hasty in thy spirit to be angry: for anger resteth in the bosom of fools."; In Proverbs 14:17 "*He that is* soon angry dealeth foolishly: and a man of wicked devices is hated."; and in Proverbs 14:29 "*He that is* slow to wrath *is* of great understanding: but *he that is* hasty of spirit exalteth folly."

Often, anger is associated with the phrase a quick temper. One thing you often will hear people talk about in regards to anger is to count to 10 before you respond. This is actually an application of what the Bible says here about not being hasty in anger. The word hasty means rash, not deliberate, irritable, or easily excited to wrath. This is a state of mind not just a response. In other words, you must train your mind to be deliberate and at ease. You cannot live on the edge of anger and avoid falling into it. If you are going to avoid anger you must learn to control your mind rather than allow it to control you. The Bible talks about this constantly. It gives a pattern for this in Philippians 4:4-8, "Rejoice in the Lord alway: and again I say, Rejoice. Let your moderation be known unto all men. The Lord is at hand. Be careful for nothing; but in every thing by prayer and supplication with thanksgiving let your requests be made known unto God. And the peace of God, which passeth all understanding, shall keep your hearts and minds through Christ Jesus. Finally, brethren, whatsoever things are true, whatsoever things are honest, whatsoever things are just, whatsoever things are pure, whatsoever things are lovely, whatsoever things are of good report; if there be any virtue, and if there be any praise, think on these things."

Notice the process here:

1. Develop a positive outlook through praise.

2. Practice having a moderate spirit so that others can see you are not hasty or rash.
3. Exercise thankfulness in your life through prayer.
4. Keep your mind stayed on that which is good rather than that which is bad.

Do you notice how much thanksgiving and praise are a part of having a mind that is controlled rather than one that is rash? Remember how the issue of ingratitude results from exercising anger? If you are going to develop a mind that is free from hast to anger you can begin with doing what we call a **stroke file**. This is a tool to help you gain victory over negative thinking. Take a 3x5 card each morning and write the date in the top right corner. On the left write A.M, Noon, P.M.; on each of these occasions write 3 things that you can see to thank God for. On the back write one thing you can be thankful for about the person you struggle with anger the most with. This process will help you keep a mind that is content rather than one looking for offence at every turn.

Another tool that will help you in slowing down anger is to do what we call a **trigger list**. Keep a small notebook in your pocket or purse. When you get angry make a record of it with date and time. Write down the event that stirred up anger and then a short evaluation of the real reason you are angry. What I mean by that is separate the action from the reason. The action may have been that someone spoke rudely to you but the reason for your anger is internal not external so take a real evaluation, I expect people to be polite. Here we identify the real issue, our expectation. Thus, we can identify and move on. As you do this you will possible find that there are certain times of the day that you struggle with anger more than others, there may be certain things that stimulate anger more than others and as you make this determination you can plan against allowing anger to control you by either modifying your day or preparing against such stimulus.

I want to address for a moment also what to do about the troubling thoughts concerning anger. To do this I want you to look at James 4:6-10, "But he giveth more grace. Wherefore he saith, God resisteth the proud, but giveth grace unto the humble. 7 Submit yourselves therefore to God. Resist the devil, and he will flee from you. 8 Draw nigh to God, and he will draw nigh to you. Cleanse your hands, ye sinners; and purify your hearts, ye double minded. 9 Be afflicted, and mourn, and weep: let your laughter be turned to mourning, and your joy to heaviness. 10 Humble yourselves in the sight of the Lord, and he shall lift you up."

Please do not discount the fact that the Devil loves to keep people trapped in anger, as a matter of fact it says in 2 Corinthians 2:10-11, "To whom ye forgive any thing, I forgive also: for if I forgave any thing, to whom I forgave it, for your sakes forgave I it in the person of Christ; 11 Lest Satan should get an advantage of us: for we are not ignorant of his devices." When you are giving into anger, you are actually falling prey to demonic devices. The Bible warns of this at least twice. In order then for you to resist the demonic aspect of anger you must resist this device as it teaches in James 4. The way to do this is to draw close to God. Consider how this works as illustrated in the following diagram.

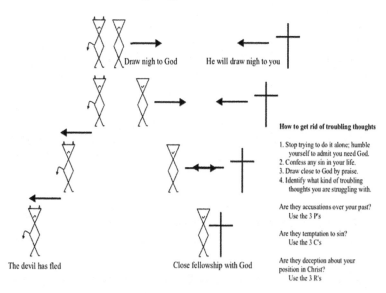

Draw nigh to God   He will draw nigh to you

How to get rid of troubling thoughts

1. Stop trying to do it alone; humble yourself to admit you need God.
2. Confess any sin in your life.
3. Draw close to God by praise.
4. Identify what kind of troubling thoughts you are struggling with.

Are they accusations over your past? Use the 3 P's

Are they temptation to sin? Use the 3 C's

Are they deception about your position in Christ? Use the 3 R's

The devil has fled   Close fellowship with God

The second way to deal with the troubling thoughts that are brought by anger is found in Revelation 12:7-11, "And there was war in heaven: Michael and his angels fought against the dragon; and the dragon fought and his angels, 8 And prevailed not; neither was their place found any more in heaven. 9 And the great dragon was cast out, that old serpent, called the Devil, and Satan, which deceiveth the whole world: he was cast out into the earth, and his angels were cast out with him. 10 And I heard a loud voice saying in heaven, Now is come salvation, and strength, and the kingdom of our God, and the power of his Christ: for the accuser of our brethren is cast down, which accused them before our God day and night. 11 And they overcame him by the blood of the Lamb, and by the word of their testimony; and they loved not their lives unto the death."

This process of dealing with troubling thoughts we call the 3 P's. Notice here that it calls the devil the accuser of the brethren. He constantly accuses us before God, but he is also constantly accusing us to ourselves and others before us as well. The way that they overcame him in this text is simple. First by the blood of the Lamb, we will call this Pleading the blood. The second step is the word of their testimony, we will call that Praising the Lord. The third step is that they loved not their lives to the death, we will call that Practicing the truth.

If you will do these three things when the Accuser attacks you then you will gain victory also. Begin by pleading the blood against the accusation, either by confessing the sin to God or by reminding God that it has been confessed and covered by the blood of Jesus Christ. Then begin to praise God for everything that He has done for you and everything that you can see. Give God thanks and praise Him until the evil spirit of accusation departs from your heart. Finally do what you know God has called you to do. That is what we call practicing the truth. When you first start this practice, the Devil will probably attack you more to try and keep you from establishing this as a habit because He knows that if you do then you will have victory over his accusations. Don't let him stop you, push through his onslaught and you will have great victory over the old accusations that he has used to keep you down. These truths are illustrated in the following diagram.

3 P's
Revelation 12:7-11

P/P/P
You are in spiritual warfare!
2 Cor. 10:4

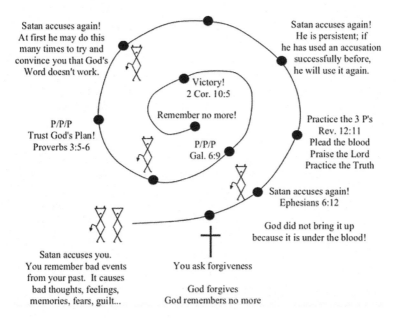

Satan accuses again!
At first he may do this
many times to try and
convince you that God's
Word doesn't work.

Satan accuses again!
He is persistent; if
he has used an accusation
successfully before,
he will use it again.

Victory!
2 Cor. 10:5

Remember no more!

P/P/P
Trust God's Plan!
Proverbs 3:5-6

Practice the 3 P's
Rev. 12:11
Plead the blood
Praise the Lord
Practice the Truth

P/P/P
Gal. 6:9

Satan accuses again!
Ephesians 6:12

God did not bring it up
because it is under the blood!

Satan accuses you.
You remember bad events
from your past. It causes
bad thoughts, feelings,
memories, fears, guilt...

You ask forgiveness

God forgives
God remembers no more

51

Learn to exercise discretion and prudence – Proverbs 19:11, "The discretion of a man deferreth his anger; and *it is* his glory to pass over a transgression." Proverbs 12:16 "A fool's wrath is presently known: but a prudent *man* covereth shame." According to the Webster's 1828 dictionary discretion is that discernment which enables a person to judge critically what is correct and proper, discretion should be united with caution. In other words, discretion is to be cautious, not to act quickly without exercising proper judgment as to what would be the proper response. Prudence according to the same dictionary implies "a caution in deliberating and consulting on the most suitable means to accomplish valuable purposes. Prudence is principally in reference to actions to be done and the due means, order, season and method in doing or not doing them."

When a problem comes in your life you have generally responded in one of two ways. You have either externalized by blowing up taking our anger out on those around you including your spouse and children. Or you have internalized your anger allowing it to build up causing you to have increasing emotional stress. Both of these methods are bad because they either kill your relationships or they kill you. The real answer to this is found in the admonition to discretion and prudence. You must learn to deal with the problem. The problem is never an individual, it is the beliefs that are motivating them. Consider the illustration on the next page.

Anger
Ephesians 4:26-27

There are 3 ways to deal with anger

1. Internalize the anger

This build up of anger is anger turned inward.

This produces
1. Despair
2. Despondency
3. Discouragement
4. Depression
5. Death wishes

2. Ventilate the anger

This explosion of anger is anger turned outward.

This produces
1. Destroyed relationships
2. Delusion that problems
   were solved
3. Dependence on anger as
   a coping mechanism

Ventilation is sin

Proverbs 14:17; 14:19; 15:18; 19:11; 19:19; 22:24-25; 25:28; 29:11; 29:20;

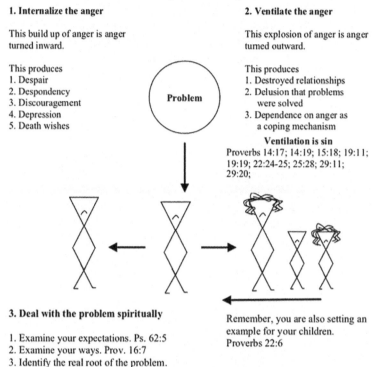

3. Deal with the problem spiritually

1. Examine your expectations. Ps. 62:5
2. Examine your ways. Prov. 16:7
3. Identify the real root of the problem.
   Attack the problem not the people.
   It is not what was done, but why it
   was done. Mark 7:21-23
4. Use Biblical communication to
   approach the problem. Matt. 6:9-13
5. Be kind, tenderhearted and forgive.
   Eph. 4:31-32
6 Maintain a Spirit-filled life. Gal. 5:16

Remember, you are also setting an example for your children.
Proverbs 22:6

If you are going to gain victory over the problem, you must separate the problem from the individual and evaluate what it is they are doing that is actually causing your anger. Then you must deal with that issue. To do this you most likely will need to express the problem to them in a way that they will receive it. That means that you must not attack them with accusations about the issue. This will only cause them to become defensive and protect themselves from change. To help others see the need to change you need to employ that techniques that Jesus taught us when He taught how to pray.

It says in Matthew 6:9-13 "After this manner therefore pray ye: Our Father which art in heaven, Hallowed be thy name. Thy kingdom come. Thy will be done in earth, as it is in heaven. Give us this day our daily bread. And forgive us our debts, as we forgive our debtors. And lead us not into temptation, but deliver us from evil: For thine is the kingdom, and the power, and the glory, for ever. Amen." Without going into a full lesson on this I will outline just the basic format for you.

1. Begin with a positive comment of praise for the individual.
2. Ask if there is anything that you can do to assist them.
3. Make your request for their help.
4. Ask for and extend forgiveness for past conflicts.
5. End with a positive statement.

Practice the put off/put on principle - Ephesians 4:31-32, "Let all bitterness, and wrath, and anger, and clamour, and evil speaking, be put away from you, with all malice: And be ye kind one to another, tenderhearted, forgiving one another, even as God for Christ's sake hath forgiven you." If you are going to get long term victory over anger you must put the right practices in its place so that it has no room to come back in. To illustrate this, I want you to consider this drawing.

Put Off/ Put On
How to restructure a life through repentance and replacement
Ephesians 4:20-24

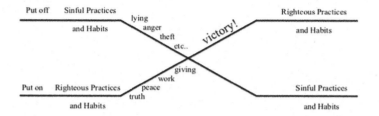

The 3 part process the Bible teaches is
1. Identify the sinful action
2. Identify the Biblical practice
3. Renew the mind to change your thinking

Considering our topic, we see the negative actions listed in Ephesians 4:31, bitterness, wrath, anger, clamour (repeated loud outbursts), evil speaking (talking bad about someone or something, and malice (intent to do harm). In order to put these things off you are to put in their place what is listed in verse 32. Kindness, tenderheartedness and forgiveness. Let's extend on this issue of forgiveness for just a moment.

There are basically 3 options for forgiveness that are practiced. One is logical forgiveness, this means that you forgive because it makes sense to forgive. It would be bad for you if you didn't forgive and thus the reasonable thing to do is let it go and move on. The problem with this is that eventually it doesn't make sense any more. This is what Peter was questioning when He asked Jesus how often should I forgive my brother, is seven times enough? Jesus blew Peter's mind when He said, seven times seventy. Let's be honest tonight the idea of forgiving someone seven times for the same offence is far more than what most of us would be willing to do. I think the rule in America is three strikes you're out. There does come a point where forgiveness doesn't make logical sense.

The second type of forgiveness is emotional forgiveness, that is I feel like forgiving. I don't feel like being angry anymore, so I am going to just let it go and forgive. The issue here is that feelings also change. This is why I heard a man say once that when his wife got angry at him she became historical, she brought up everything he had ever done. She felt like forgiving him at the time, but she didn't feel like it at that time. Emotional forgiveness doesn't work any better than logical forgiveness.

The only type of forgiveness that actually works is spiritual forgiveness and that is what Paul was speaking about in Ephesians 4:32. He said there forgive even as God for Christ sake has forgiven you. Notice that God's forgiveness is not based upon his thinking or feelings, it is based upon the action of Jesus Christ dying on the cross to pay for sin. It is a legislative forgiveness. It counts the payment of Christ sufficient to cover any offence. When a person comes to God and asks forgiveness He doesn't have to think about it, He doesn't weigh how He feels about them or what they have done, He has already made up His mind that He will extend forgiveness to everyone for everything based upon the fixed and never changing basis of Christ dying on the cross to pay the penalty of sin.

Paul admonishes us that the way we are to forgive is the same way that God Himself forgives. We are to base all our forgiveness on the cross of Christ. Paul says in 2 Corinthians 2:10, "To whom ye forgive any thing, I forgive also: for if I forgave any thing, to whom I forgave it, for your sakes forgave I it in the person of Christ;" Paul's personal experience with forgiveness was based upon this same principle, he forgave others in the person of Christ. This is to say, when I consider the offence I compare it to what Christ did to forgive me and I choose Him over my offences. Certainly, my own sin that cost Jesus Christ His life on the cross was far more severe than any individual offence that could be committed against me. The Bible says that Jesus bore all of our sin in His own body on the cross. He died for every one of my sins, He died for all the lies in the world, all the murders, all the rapes, all the thefts, all the adulteries and idolatries. All of these things were put on Him while He was on the cross and He made the choice to pay the penalty for them.

After the model prayer Jesus makes the following dramatic statement, "For if ye forgive men their trespasses, your heavenly

Father will also forgive you: 15 But if ye forgive not men their trespasses, neither will your Father forgive your trespasses." Matthew 6:14-15 God says that an individual receiving forgiveness from Him is dependent upon them extending forgiveness to others in the same fashion. Here is why, how could you rightly say that you deserve God's forgiveness and others do not? To refuse to extend the same forgiveness that you have received is to despise the sacrifice of Jesus Christ for the payment of sin. truly they do not deserve forgiveness, but neither do you. God's forgiveness was not based upon deserving it, it was based upon His love. God loved you so much that He was willing to pay the penalty for your sin Himself on the cross. This is the message of the gospel.

Let me say, if you have never acknowledged your sin before God and put your faith in Jesus Christ for the forgiveness of your sin then you are still responsible for the payment of your sin. God wants to forgive you, He has paid the price to forgive you, but you must accept that forgiveness that He has offered. It says in Romans 10:8-10, "But what saith it? The word is nigh thee, even in thy mouth, and in thy heart: that is, the word of faith, which we preach; 9 That if thou shalt confess with thy mouth the Lord Jesus, and shalt believe in thine heart that God hath raised him from the dead, thou shalt be saved. 10 For with the heart man believeth unto righteousness; and with the mouth confession is made unto salvation."

You cannot give something you have never received yourself, and once you have received God's forgiveness you would not be able to refuse it to others.

Never hold onto things - Ephesians 4:26 "Be ye angry, and sin not: let not the sun go down upon your wrath:" The last admonition that I want you to see on overcoming anger is that you cannot hold onto things and maintain victory over anger. When the Bible says here "don't let the sun go down upon your wrath", it is saying, deal with it properly today instead of letting it fester into resentment and bitterness. Remember that is the process that took Cain down the road to destruction. The practical action of letting things go is found in a daily choice for forgiveness. If you will follow the steps that we have outlined here, you will not have the problem of holding onto grudges.

Exercise: Make a list below of the steps that you have learned here that you need to take action on and write out a plan to put them into practice.

_____
_____
_____
_____
_____
_____
_____
_____
_____
_____
_____
_____
_____
_____
_____
_____
_____
_____
_____
_____
_____
_____

Seven

Maintaining Victory Over Anger

Simply put, the only way to maintain victory over anger is to consistently walk in the Spirit. Paul discusses this in the following passage.

> Galatians 5:16-21 "This I say then, Walk in the Spirit, and ye shall not fulfil the lust of the flesh. For the flesh lusteth against the Spirit, and the Spirit against the flesh: and these are contrary the one to the other: so that ye cannot do the things that ye would. But if ye be led of the Spirit, ye are not under the law. Now the works of the flesh are manifest, which are these; Adultery, fornication, uncleanness, lasciviousness, Idolatry, witchcraft, hatred, variance, emulations, wrath, strife, seditions, heresies, Envyings, murders, drunkenness, revellings, and such like: of the which I tell you before, as I have also told you in time past, that they which do such things shall not inherit the kingdom of God."

Notice here that walking in the Spirit is said to be the opposite of fulfilling the lusts of your flesh. Giving into anger as we have already learned is, by definition, fulfilling the lusts of the flesh. The only way then to prevent fulfilling the lust of your flesh to give into anger is to walk continually in the Spirit.

Walking in the Spirit is no magic or mystical thing, however. It is simply the result of having a consistent walk with God Himself. Most people reading this book have been told countless times to read their Bible and pray, yet so often we approach these things as if the activity was the goal. The reality is far from that; the activity is a means to an end in walking with God.

If I wanted to have a relationship with you, it would take more than just reading everything that you say; I would have to interact with you. I could easily read what you say to study you without ever desiring to have a relationship with you. Unfortunately, that seems to be how some approach their time in God's Word. It is very clinical for them: they don't have an interaction with God, instead they read their Bible for information. They may pray in the same manner having a "just the facts" type of prayer life.

You cannot approach your relationship with God as if He were a science project. You must approach Him with an earnest desire to know and interact with Him. God reminds us in Jeremiah 23:23 "Am I a God at hand, saith the LORD, and not a God afar off?" God is not somewhere out there watching from a distance as an old song suggests, but He is ever present with you. He wants to fellowship with you, so much so that He gave His only Begotten Son to die for your sin debt. When you accepted Christ as your Saviour, He did not simply write your name down and say see you later! No, He and the Father and the Holy Spirit moved right in with you.

This is what Jesus said in John 14:23 "Jesus answered and said unto him, "If a man love me, he will keep my words: and my Father will love him, and we will come unto him, and make our abode with him.""

Paul expresses the same thing in Romans 8:9-11, "But ye are not in the flesh, but in the Spirit, if so be that the Spirit of God dwell in you. Now if any man have not the Spirit of Christ, he is none of his. And if Christ be in you, the body is dead because of sin; but the Spirit is life because of righteousness. But if the Spirit of him that raised up Jesus from the dead dwell in you, he that raised up Christ from the dead shall also quicken your mortal bodies by his Spirit that dwelleth in you."

God is a quickening Spirit within you, and yet you treat Him as if He were a science experiment to be examined instead of fellowshipped with. He is not an impersonal force as if you were a character in Star Wars. We have a living personal God who, beyond our comprehension, has made us able to commune with Him. We do this by talking with Him in prayer, reading His Word, and listening to it preached. When we do these things, the Spirit of God communes with our Spirit. He confirms His presence within us and teaches us, pointing out what we need to know, pressing on our spirit where we need to get right, and giving direction to us in the decisions we need to make.

Walking in the Spirit isn't a place you attain to; it is a practice you keep. You don't have to be perfect to walk in the Spirit, you just have to be yielded to God. As you yield to Him, you will find areas that you need to correct and your willingness to do that keeps that fellowship consistent. When you stop responding to His leadership, you break that fellowship and are back to walking in the flesh.

Paul shows us what it looks like when a person is walking in the Spirit in Ephesians 5:18-21.

> "And be not drunk with wine, wherein is excess; but be filled with the Spirit; Speaking to yourselves in psalms and hymns and spiritual songs, singing and making melody in your heart to the Lord; Giving thanks always for all things unto God and the Father in the name of our Lord Jesus Christ; Submitting yourselves one to another in the fear of God."

There are three evidences given here to be able to judge if you are walking in the Spirit. Let me say that a different way: you should examine yourself to be sure that you are in the Spirit rather than worrying about if everyone else is. If you are in the Spirit, your response will be right, but you cannot make others be in the Spirit.

The first evidence we see of someone who is walking in the Spirit is that they will have a joyful attitude. That is expressed in the statement that those filled with the Spirit "will speak to themselves in Songs and hymns and spiritual songs, singing and making melody in their hearts to the Lord." You cannot be filled with anger and joy at the same time. You cannot be filled with anger and the praises of God at the same time, either. It doesn't say here that you will be a good singer; it says that you will have a good song in your heart. If the song of your heart is a sinful one, then you can be sure that you are not walking in the Spirit. That is not my assessment; that is what the Bible says.

The second evidence we see is that a person who is walking in the Spirit will have a thankful attitude. Do you remember that one of the consequences of anger we saw in Genesis was being ungrateful? That is not a coincidence! God has called us to walk in the Spirit, and one of the evidences of doing that is having a thankful attitude, which is the opposite of having an attitude of ingratitude. We are told in 1 Thessalonians 5:18, "In every thing give thanks: for this is the will of God in Christ Jesus concerning you." It is God's will for you to be thankful and the way that He desires for you to accomplish that is by having this attitude which is the result of walking in the Spirit.

The third evidence we see is that of having a humble attitude. It says that the person who is filled with the Spirit will submit themselves one to another in the fear of God. Anger is often the result of our pride, so it is easy to see how walking in the Spirit and having a humble attitude would be the opposite of this. Remember that we are told in James 4:6, "But he giveth more grace. Wherefore he saith, God resisteth the proud, but giveth grace unto the humble."

Much could be said about the necessity of humility, but could we not simply understand that a person who is walking in the Spirit will exhibit this attitude and a person who instead shows an attitude of pride is then not walking in the Spirit of God but in their flesh? When a person submits themselves to the Spirit of God, the spirit of pride that results from the flesh must be put away.

It is no accident that these same evidences are found in Colossians 3:16-17, which says, "Let the word of Christ dwell in you richly in all wisdom; teaching and admonishing one another in psalms and hymns and spiritual songs, singing with grace in your hearts to the Lord. And whatsoever ye do in word or deed, do all in the name of the Lord Jesus, giving thanks to God and the Father by him." This passage then goes on to tell wives to submit to their husband, husbands to love their wives, children to obey their parents, fathers not to provoke their children, and employees to obey their bosses. All these things are indicative of people who are exhibiting humility in their lives.

You see the evidences of being filled with the Spirit in Ephesians are the same as the evidences of being filled with the Word of Christ in Colossians. The issue, though, is not that of simple rote memorization of scripture. It is that of walking with God which necessarily includes being in the Word and in fact means that the Word is making its way into you. Being filled with the Word is simply a result of waking with God in a real way.

God did not make walking in the Spirit some mysterious thing. Every believer can walk in the Spirit, and if you are going to maintain victory over your anger, you must begin to do so. Don't deceive yourself into thinking that you can continue the same way you have been, and things will be different. If you haven't been exhibiting the attributes of walking in the Spirit, then you haven't been walking in the Spirit. I am not saying that you weren't saved, and that God never spoke to you through His Word at all; I am saying that there is a difference in your attitude when you are walking in the Spirit than when you are walking in the flesh. You cannot maintain victory over the flesh without walking continually in the Spirit.

Exercise: Evaluate your walk with God and determine what you need to do to begin walking in the Spirit. Write out your plan here and begin doing it immediately.

_____
_____
_____
_____

"For by grace are ye saved through faith;
and that not of yourselves: it is the gift of
God: Not of works, lest any man should
boast."
~Ephesians 2:8-9

CONQUERING YOUR ANGER

Eight

How to Restore Relationships Damaged by Anger

This brings us to our final topic how to restore relationships damaged by anger. It could be that you have made the decision to deal with your anger already and yet the effects of past episodes linger in the relationship. The reality is that unresolved conflicts from our past have a great influence on not only our current relationships but also our spiritual and emotional wellbeing. One account in the Bible gives us a good view of how to restore relationships that have been damaged by anger specifically. That story is of Joseph and his brothers.

We see the beginning of their conflict in Genesis 37:3-8

> "Now Israel loved Joseph more than all his children, because he was the son of his old age: and he made him a coat of many colours. 4 And when his brethren saw that their father loved him more than all his brethren, they hated him, and could not speak peaceably unto him. 5 And Joseph dreamed a dream, and he told it his brethren: and they hated him yet the more. 6 And he said unto them, Hear, I pray you, this dream which I have dreamed: 7

For, behold, we were binding sheaves in the field,
and, lo, my sheaf arose, and also stood upright; and,
behold, your sheaves stood round about, and made
obeisance to my sheaf. 8 And his brethren said to
him, Shalt thou indeed reign over us? or shalt thou
indeed have dominion over us? And they hated him
yet the more for his dreams, and for his words."

If you are familiar with the Biblical account, you know that because
of Joseph's brother's envy, anger and hatred toward him they
decided to get rid of him. They caught him, threw him in a pit, faked
his death and sold him into slavery. It is not likely that your anger
has ever reached that fevered of a pitch. That doesn't mean it isn't
as bad because we have already seen the effects of anger that is left
unchecked. Many years went by before Joseph saw his brothers
again and by the time he did his circumstances had changed
dramatically. Joseph was now the second in charge of the land of
Egypt and his brothers were coming to buy food because of a famine
in the land of Canaan. As we pick the narrative back up Joseph
seems to be in a conflict with how to treat his brothers who had
done so much wrong to him.

As Joseph was dealing with them they began to confess their guilt
over what they had done in Genesis 42:21-23 "And they said one to
another, We are verily guilty concerning our brother, in that we saw
the anguish of his soul, when he besought us, and we would not hear;
therefore is this distress come upon us. 22 And Reuben answered
them, saying, Spake I not unto you, saying, Do not sin against the
child; and ye would not hear? therefore, behold, also his blood is
required. 23 And they knew not that Joseph understood them; for
he spake unto them by an interpreter."

The account continues, and Joseph's brothers bring Benjamin with
them the next time they come to buy corn. This time Joseph sets
Benjamin up to be guilty of stealing his cup. When Joseph confronts
his brothers to see how they will respond he sees not only that they
have remorse over how they had treated him but that they are
resolved not to treat their youngest brother the same way. This
account transpires in Genesis 44:12-34

"12 And he searched, and began at the eldest, and left at the youngest: and the cup was found in Benjamin's sack. 13 Then they rent their clothes, and laded every man his ass, and returned to the city. 14 And Judah and his brethren came to Joseph's house; for he was yet there: and they fell before him on the ground. 15 And Joseph said unto them, What deed is this that ye have done? wot ye not that such a man as I can certainly divine? 16 And Judah said, What shall we say unto my lord? what shall we speak? or how shall we clear ourselves? God hath found out the iniquity of thy servants: behold, we are my lord's servants, both we, and he also with whom the cup is found. 17 And he said, God forbid that I should do so: but the man in whose hand the cup is found, he shall be my servant; and as for you, get you up in peace unto your father. 18 Then Judah came near unto him, and said, Oh my lord, let thy servant, I pray thee, speak a word in my lord's ears, and let not thine anger burn against thy servant: for thou art even as Pharaoh. 19 My lord asked his servants, saying, Have ye a father, or a brother? 20 And we said unto my lord, We have a father, an old man, and a child of his old age, a little one; and his brother is dead, and he alone is left of his mother, and his father loveth him. 21 And thou saidst unto thy servants, Bring him down unto me, that I may set mine eyes upon him. 22 And we said unto my lord, The lad cannot leave his father: for if he should leave his father, his father would die. 23 And thou saidst unto thy servants, Except your youngest brother come down with you, ye shall see my face no more. 24 And it came to pass when we came up unto thy servant my father, we told him the words of my lord. 25 And our father said, Go again, and buy us a little food. 26 And we said, We cannot go down: if our youngest brother be with us, then will we go down: for we may not see the man's face, except our youngest brother be with us.

27 And thy servant my father said unto us, Ye know that my wife bare me two sons: 28 And the one went out from me, and I said, Surely he is torn in pieces; and I saw him not since: 29 And if ye take this also from me, and mischief befall him, ye shall bring down my gray hairs with sorrow to the grave. 30 Now therefore when I come to thy servant my father, and the lad be not with us; seeing that his life is bound up in the lad's life; 31 It shall come to pass, when he seeth that the lad is not with us, that he will die: and thy servants shall bring down the gray hairs of thy servant our father with sorrow to the grave. 32 For thy servant became surety for the lad unto my father, saying, If I bring him not unto thee, then I shall bear the blame to my father for ever. 33 Now therefore, I pray thee, let thy servant abide instead of the lad a bondman to my lord; and let the lad go up with his brethren. 34 For how shall I go up to my father, and the lad be not with me? lest peradventure I see the evil that shall come on my father."

It is at this point that Joseph knows that there has indeed been a change in his brothers and he reveals himself to them and forgives them. It says in Genesis 45:4-5

"And Joseph said unto his brethren, Come near to me, I pray you. And they came near. And he said, I am Joseph your brother, whom ye sold into Egypt. 5 Now therefore be not grieved, nor angry with yourselves, that ye sold me hither: for God did send me before you to preserve life."

I want to take a few minutes now and draw together the picture here about repairing relationships damaged by anger based upon this account. There are elements that are shown here on both sides that are important to account for. Let's begin with on the side of the offending party, the one who acted in anger. Two dynamics stand out in regards to them. First, they demonstrated a genuine remorse. So often people who have acted in anger apologize only when asked.

This often makes them seem insincere. Acknowledgement of your wrong only when confronted by it has an air of self service to it. Thus, if you are going to begin to repair a relationship you must unilaterally accept responsibility for your actions and the damage they caused. In the Biblical account this happened because they did not know that they were talking to Joseph. In your situation it would probably be best to do so in the form of a letter. This avoids the point of argument and allows you to fully express genuine remorse for your actions and the harm they have caused. When writing such a letter, do not in any fashion justify what you have done. Accept full responsibility and detail what harms you know you have caused. Ask for them to show you mercy as you attempt to demonstrate that you have indeed changed.

The second important aspect that Joseph saw in his brothers was an actual demonstration that they had changed. Someone who is truly repentive of their wrong changed. The Psalmist King David said in Psalm 55:19b "Because they have no changes, therefore they fear not God." True repentance from wrong actions is revealed in what kind of changes we have made. Do not get angry when those you have hurt do not just take your word for it that you are sorry or that you have changed. You have demonstrated one behavior for them now you must demonstrate a new behavior. Besides, you getting angry because they don't believe you actually itself demonstrates that nothing has changed.

The alternate side of this equation is the one who has been wronged. In this Bible account that person is Joseph. There are two things that we see about Joseph which are important as well. First, Joseph was willing to take an honest look at the situation and not allow his past bias to prevent reconciliation. So often those who have been hurt are not willing to accept that others have changed. I am not saying that you should put on rose colored glasses. I am saying that you must have an open heart to honestly examine the situation. I know that often the statement is given that "people don't change". I want you to ask a different question, can God change people? On their own they might well not change but if you believe the Bible at all you must acknowledge that God can indeed change people. The Holy Spirit living in their life can make a change. I experienced that change, I went from being an angry person to yielding my spirit to

God. That was not a salvation experience it was a surrender experience. I was already saved, I had just never surrendered my anger to God. once I did, there was a decided difference in me, one that was made by God himself.

The second element that Joseph shows in this account is that He forgave. At some point if you have been offended you must practice forgiveness. As we spoke before about forgiveness this is important not only for the relationship but also for your own spiritual life. When forgiveness meets repentance there is restoration. That is the example in our text and that is also the example presented by our own relationship to God. You see, we had offended against God's law and in defiance of His commandment rebelled against Him. Yet the Bible says in Romans 5:10 "For if, when we were enemies, we were reconciled to God by the death of his Son, much more, being reconciled, we shall be saved by his life."

That word reconciled is an interesting word, it is used repeatedly to describe our relationship to God once we have received Christ as our Saviour. It says in Colossians 1:21 "And you, that were sometime alienated and enemies in your mind by wicked works, yet now hath he reconciled" God sought a reconciliation with us and knew that the payment for sin must be made, however He did something amazing, He made it Himself. Now let me tie this back to what we are talking about specifically. The offended party is not to expect repayment for the wrong done to them. God has clearly shown that there is no way that we could ever pay for our sin debt, there is no way that we could ever earn our way to heaven, He specifically says in Ephesians 2:8-9 "For by grace are ye saved through faith; and that not of yourselves: it is the gift of God: 9 Not of works, lest any man should boast." Forgiveness is not about restitution, it is about repentance. God was willing to reconcile and thus He extended the offer of mercy for what we had done and grace to renew a right relationship with Him. That is the same spirit that He asks us to have toward those who have wronged us.

Another interesting factor in the Biblical example of restitution is the mediator. That meaning that in both the Bible teaching concerning our reconciliation toward God and Joseph's toward his brothers, the offended individual acted as a mediator to the situation. Joseph was able to do this because he had changed so much since the last time he had seen his brothers. God did this in the person of Christ. It says in 2 Corinthians 5:19 "To wit, that God was in Christ, reconciling the world unto himself, not imputing their trespasses unto them; and hath committed unto us the word of reconciliation." God sent Jesus Christ to be the mediator of a covenant to reconcile our relationship to Himself. There was no one else that could have been such a mediator.

That being said, God has also asked all believers to involve themselves in this process of reconciliation by being witnesses of the fact that He is willing and able to forgive us for our offences. It says in 2 Corinthians 5:20 "Now then we are ambassadors for Christ, as though God did beseech you by us: we pray you in Christ's stead, be ye reconciled to God." It also says in Galatians 6:1 "Brethren, if a man be overtaken in a fault, ye which are spiritual, restore such an one in the spirit of meekness; considering thyself, lest thou also be tempted." Thus, there is a Biblical example that if you as an offended party are willing to be spiritually affected toward forgiveness you should get another brother or sister to act as a mediator for you to approach the offender and offer terms of reconciliation. Such terms must not require restitution as such, but must include a demonstration of remorse and example of change. Restoration is not possible without repentance so if they are not sorry for what they have done and willing to demonstrate that they have indeed changed then such restoration should be put on hold until that time comes. God, likewise, has offered forgiveness and restoration to all men but only such as come to Him through faith in Jesus Christ receive such reconciliation. This is as such an example for us to follow in renewing relationships with those who have wronged us.

I hope that this book has been a help to you and opened your eyes not only to the dangers of anger and how to overcome it but also to how to deal with others who are affected by anger and restore relationships that have been damaged.

Exercise: Write out what you need to do to begin restoring the relationships that you have damaged by your anger.

Nine

How to Deal with an Angry Person

Anger is such a prevalent issue in our day there is no way to avoid dealing with angry people. The Bible gives 10 direct answers to dealing with an angry person that can be divided into three general categories.

1. What your personal response should be
2. How to defuse an immediate situation.
3. What the long term solution for dealing with a habitually angry person is.

Let's begin with your personal response to an angry person.

Be slow to anger - Proverbs 15:18 "A wrathful man stirreth up strife: but *he that is* slow to anger appeaseth strife."; Proverbs 16:32 "*He that is* slow to anger *is* better than the mighty; and he that ruleth his spirit than he that taketh a city." Often the worst response to anger is to respond in kind. The problem is not resolved by this reaction and the issue usually escalates quickly because two angry people can do far more damage than one. Having control over your own spirit is vital if you are going to deal with an angry person because the moment you lose your own temper you lose the ability to change the situation.

Listen and don't answer quickly - James 1:19 "Wherefore, my beloved brethren, let every man be swift to hear, slow to speak, slow to wrath:" One of the most important non-Bible statements I have ever heard is "listen to understand, not to respond." So many times, when confronted by an angry person we let their tone outweigh their words and we respond to their attitude instead of their issue. If you are going to deal with an angry person you must listen fully to the words they are saying and detach from the tone they are said in. If you cannot understand the issue they have, let them know that you want to help but need further clarification.

Do not provoke them - Proverbs 20:2 "The fear of a king *is* as the roaring of a lion: *whoso* provoketh him to anger sinneth *against* his own soul." To provoke means to stimulate toward something. In this instance it is to stimulate someone toward anger. Twice in the Bible it warns fathers not to provoke their children to anger. The idea there is that we are not to stimulate anger in them, or in anyone. Stimulating anger in someone may be through them seeing it in us. Provoking anger could also be as simple as giving a smart-aleck answer. When someone is angry it is not the time to show how witty you are. Provoking them could be instigating an issue with someone you know struggles with anger, it could be poking at an area that you know they struggle with. All of these things must be avoided if you are going to stem the angry response. Provoking anger is a serious issue with God. Many times, in the Bible we are warned not to cause strife and contention, this is the idea of provoking.

Give a soft answer - Proverbs 15:1 "A soft answer turneth away wrath: but grievous words stir up anger." This would basically be the opposite of provoking. A soft answer is one of understanding and compassion. It is the result of listening fully to understand a person's problem and having a heart to help them. Often, we are guilty of selfishness and fail to be a help to others in need. A great example of this verse is the account in the Old Testament of Nabal and Abigail. David had watched over the flocks and herdsmen of Nabal and when he was in need he asked for Nabal to provide his men some food. Nabal had a harsh answer to David even though David had protected his herds. Nabal's words stirred up David in anger. David because of his anger thought to come and fight against Nabal but Abigail, Nabal's wife heard about it and sent a gift to

David along with a message of kindness about how he had protected their herds. She asked him to forgive the rude comments of her husband and it was her soft answer that turned David's heart away from anger. It reminds me of the verse in Proverbs 18:21 "Death and life are in the power of the tongue: and they that love it shall eat the fruit thereof." Nabal's words were to death, provoking anger. Abigail's words were to life, turning away anger. It is so important that we weigh our words.

Next let's consider what to do if the personal responses don't work to deal with someone's anger. If they persist in anger there are three responses given in the Bible on how to defuse the immediate situation. The first of these is always applicable and certainly the right policy in every situation. The last two of these are temporary measures only and not long term fixes, however, often in the heat of the moment you need something to change the dynamic of the situation and that is exactly what these verses give us.

Make peace - Psalm 2:12 "Kiss the Son, lest he be angry, and ye perish *from* the way, when his wrath is kindled but a little. Blessed *are* all they that put their trust in him." This is an admonition to take heed to when someone is just starting to get angry. Kiss the son means try to make peace before it goes too far. Now this verse has a very definite Messianic implication, but it also has a direct application to our conversation today. To make peace means that both sides willingly lay down their arms and come together in unity. It means there is no more quarrel to be angry about.

Other admonitions in the Bible include Romans 14:19 "Let us therefore follow after the things which make for peace, and things wherewith one may edify another."

Psalm 34:14 "Depart from evil, and do good; seek peace, and pursue it."

1 Peter 3:10-11 "For he that will love life, and see good days, let him refrain his tongue from evil, and his lips that they speak no guile: 11 Let him eschew evil, and do good; let him seek peace, and ensue it."

So, we are told to do things that make for peace, to seek peace, to pursue peace and to ensue peace, which means to follow it. Jesus said in Matthew 5:9 "Blessed are the peacemakers: for they shall be called the children of God." Ecclesiastes tells us that there is a time for everything under the sun including a time for war, but we are generally far too eager for war and far less willing for peace. A peacemaker is someone who seeks solutions rather than conflicts. Someone, who far from being passive is actively seeking solutions to problems for others.

Now we get into the areas of temporary solution. This is only if they will not consider terms of peace and you must defuse the situation.

Pacify them - Proverbs 16:14 "The wrath of a king *is as* messengers of death: but a wise man will pacify it." The word pacify means to appease, in other words, give them what they want. As I said this is not a long term solution but to defuse an immediate problem this a temporary fix. Often you will see this tactic employed with a child in the store. They start to throw a fit and in order to stop it the parent just gives them what they want. It stops the issue temporarily. The problem here is twofold. First, it requires the individual that has the ability to give them what they want to be humble enough to do it. Sometimes our pride raises up and says, "You know what? I could do that, but I am not going to just because of your attitude." Just speaking from personal experience that is what I am most prone to. The second issue is that it will set a terrible precedent if a long term solution is not addressed in the future. Thus, any time this is employed as a tactic the underlying issue must be addressed in the near future to avoid making it a common process. Let me say that often this is a poor choice when dealing within your home but can be a good choice when dealing with strangers in public such as in a business setting with an angry customer. One angry customer can turn away many potential customers. This is an appropriate time to seek to pacify someone.

Give a gift - Proverbs 21:14 "A gift in secret pacifieth anger: and a reward in the bosom strong wrath." This is a principle that many restaurants use, if they mess up your order they will quickly come around and let you know that your meal was free or give you a gift certificate for something. They have learned that it is better to do that than to lose you as a customer or have you go around talking bad about them. You may never use them again but when asked about it you will have to say that they gave you a free gift and thus the situation becomes a positive one for them. This is more than just pacifying someone it is going beyond what they have asked for and giving them something extra. Here again, it is a valuable tool when there is an immediate situation but not one that individually you could maintain every time someone gets angry at you personally. In certain situations, it may be useful and then a long term solution must be implemented.

There are 3 long term solutions that the Bible gives for dealing with people who get angry on a repeated basis. This is for those whom you have to pacify or give a gift to in order to calm them down. There is nowhere in the Bible that it says that you must subject yourself to someone's anger. As a matter of fact, we talked in the last session about forgiveness, but you must understand the distinction between forgiveness and restoration. God offers forgiveness to all men but there is no restoration of our relationship with God until we repent of sin and turn to Him. It is our repentance that produces the restored relationship. Likewise, when someone has a constant anger problem to continue that relationship on the basis that you are supposed to forgive them is only putting yourself in the position of being hurt. If they refuse to change their angry ways, then these are the admonitions to follow.

Get away from them – 2 times it says the same thing, Proverbs 21:19 "*It is* better to dwell in the wilderness, than with a contentious and an angry woman."; Then it says in Proverbs 22:24, "Make no friendship with an angry man; and with a furious man thou shalt not go:" It doesn't matter if it is an angry woman or an angry man, God says if they will not change get away from them. I am not advocating divorce, I do not believe that is ever God's will but God certainly gives us a principle of separation when someone will not deal with their sinful behavior. If it comes to this point then you must tell them, "as long as you insist on dealing in anger I will not stay around you". If that makes them mad so be it but you do not have to subject yourself to their rage. I want to point out that if any spouse ever crosses the line in anger to violence you should immediately separate yourself and not return until they have adequately demonstrated that they have dealt with their anger in a Biblical way and have changed their behavior by more than just a promise to do so, but by consistent example before you in public and private before you return home. In such instances as this has happened all legal means necessary to ensure your safety or the safety of children should be taken.

Never justify someone's anger as though it will change, it will not unless they face it, and the truth is, that some people will never deal with their anger in the right way. To put yourself in harm's way is just as foolish as standing on the railroad tracks and wishing the train were a plane.

Turn them away - Proverbs 29:8 "Scornful men bring a city into a snare: but wise *men* turn away wrath." If you must remove yourself from the company of another person because of their anger, do not have lengthy discussions about alternate issues. The only issue that they need to address is how they are going to fix their anger problem before anything else can be dealt with. You cannot resolve side issues without dealing with the main problem. Angry people are masters at diversion, they are great at convincing others that the anger was actually not their fault, or that they were justified in their anger. If this side issue was not there, then I would not be angry. Those are lies and must not be accepted. Turn them away until they deal with the root problem of anger.

Pray for them - 1 Timothy 2:8 "I will therefore that men pray every where, lifting up holy hands, without wrath and doubting." The way to pray is what the Bible calls a hedge of thorns. This is first introduced in Job1:6-12

> "Now there was a day when the sons of God came to present themselves before the LORD, and Satan came also among them. 7 And the LORD said unto Satan, Whence comest thou? Then Satan answered the LORD, and said, From going to and fro in the earth, and from walking up and down in it. 8 And the LORD said unto Satan, Hast thou considered my servant Job, that there is none like him in the earth, a perfect and an upright man, one

that feareth God, and escheweth evil? 9 Then Satan answered the LORD, and said, Doth Job fear God for nought? 10 Hast not thou made an hedge about him, and about his house, and about all that he hath on every side? thou hast blessed the work of his hands, and his substance is increased in the land. 11 But put forth thine hand now, and touch all that he hath, and he will curse thee to thy face. 12 And the LORD said unto Satan, Behold, all that he hath is in thy power; only upon himself put not forth thine hand. So Satan went forth from the presence of the LORD."

There is a wonderful promise shown here in the midst of this account. The promise is that God protects His children and the devil cannot do just whatever he wants to us. God does allow at times trials and attacks to prove us and or to strengthen us but the devil cannot go beyond what God allows. Now that being said, we see Job here is protected by this hedge from God. God allows the devil to affect a part of Job's life but not take his life. We see another account of a hedge in the book of Hosea. Hosea was a prophet that God told to marry a prostitute. He did and had 3 children. The names of his children were very telling about their relationship because the name of the first meant "my child" the name of the second meant "I am not sure" and the name of the third meant "this one isn't mine". His wife left him and went after her lovers and Hosea said, "I will withdraw my corn and my wine and hedge up her way so that she will see it was better for her with me than with her lovers." He began to pray this hedge around her that she wouldn't find pleasure in her sin, that she would have trouble from her decisions and that she would come to the place of repentance. Guess what, that happened?

I have seen people who were separated and even divorced for several years begin to pray this kind of prayer and it worked. If you have a spouse or child who is separated because of anger from you, then you should be praying a hedge of protection around them. It would go something like this, "Dear Lord, I ask that you would place a hedge of thorns around my loved one, that they would see how destructive their anger is and how it is hurting them. I pray that they would suffer the consequences of their anger so that they will see the need to change. Help them to humble themselves to you and see that it would be better for them if they gave up this anger than to keep it." You would pray that out loud for them as often as you think of them and the problem. In many ways this is also putting the devil on notice that you are getting God involved and often it works in a very quick fashion.

Exercise: Evaluate how you have been dealing with those in your life that are angry and write out what you should change based upon the Bible principals you have learned here.

_____
_____
_____
_____
_____
_____
_____
_____
_____
_____
_____
_____
_____
_____
_____
_____
_____
_____
_____
_____
_____
_____
_____
_____
_____
_____
_____
_____
_____
_____

Other books by this author

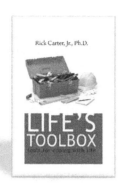

Life's Toolbox: Day after day the trials and burdens of life can become overwhelming if you don't have the proper tools to fix the problems as they arise. Life's toolbox is filled with the biblical tools that we each need to cope with life. 2 Peter 1:3 tells us, "According as his divine power hath given unto us all things that *pertain* unto life and godliness, through the knowledge of him that hath called us to glory and virtue:" We can take heart that there is not a trial or problem that we will encounter that God has not given us the answer for. So pick up your spiritual tool box and go to work. Remember that, "Ye are of God, little children, and have overcome them: be- cause greater is he that is in you, than he that is in the world." I John 4:4

The Authority Principle: Under-standing and practicing Authority according to the Bible is without doubt vital to successful and biblical living. Authority is one of the few things in life that affects every living soul. Whether the poor child in

a remote Amazonian village or the President of the United States of America, there are God given and established Authorities that govern our lives. Unfortunately, we live in a culture of independence that has fostered a rebellion to earthly authority and ultimately rebellion against God. A Biblical understanding of Authority is the key to growing in faith and having the peace of God in your life. The Authority Principle is an in-depth study on authority and God's intended place for it in our lives. These truths properly applied are sure to make a total difference in God's people and churches everywhere.

The Changing of the Garb: Putting off the Old Man and Putting on the New Man is not some mystical process that is reserved only for a select few, the tools to accomplish this transformation are given to each of us if we will apply them. There is a great disconnect between the average Christian and

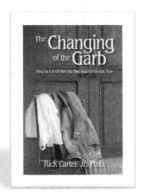

the victory that God has promised us in His Word over sin. Many people are stuck in the repentance cycle spending every day feeling as a failure in their Christian walk. The repentance cycle is that process where we continue to fall into a besetting sin despite seeking God in repentance and confession. Many have all but given up on trying to gain victory over the sins that they face and have been convinced that there is no hope for them. This book will provide you practical and usable tools to end the repentance cycle in your life and give you the knowledge from God's Word to live the victorious Christian life that you have longed for.

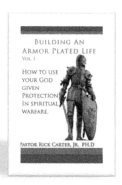

Building an Armor Plated Life volumes 1 & 2: Do you constantly feel defeated? Have you almost given up hope of victory over the constant attacks of the enemy? You are not alone. Many Christians are in the same place and the reason is that most have never been taught how to put on their spiritual armor. Having protection is not the same as using it. In These books you will learn about the armor that God has provided for His children's defense and how to use it. Victory is within your grasp as a believer and God has designed for you to live a victorious life. He has provided you with everything you need, but you must put your armor on to experience the joy God intended for you.

Knowing Him Discipleship: Far too often in churches today, discipleship is either non-existent, severely lacking, or to the opposite extreme has been made the primary focus trumping out evangelism and outreach. Jesus included the

ministry of discipleship as a vital part of a church's work in fulfilling the great commission.

The Knowing Him discipleship training curriculum is structured in such a way as to take a person from no knowledge of salvation, through being grounded in the fundamental doctrine of the Word of God, to a working servant hood in which the convert is actively winning others to Christ and investing in themselves in discipling new converts they have won.

This course is predicated on a daily study through the Word of God and a weekly meeting at which the teacher expounds the information the disciple has studied in previous week using the Knowing Him Teacher's Guide. By using this curriculum, we can see the beauty of the great commission fulfilled in our churches as the masses are won to Christ, taught to observe His teachings, and winning others as well.

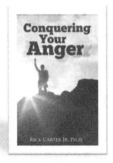

Conquering Your Anger: Are you frequently angry or do you know someone who is? Chances are you said yes to one of those two possibilities. Anger is a destructive force in the life of many people. In this book, Dr. Carter takes a look at the source of anger and how to deal with it from a Biblical manner. Too often anger is justified and excused instead of dealt with properly. You don't need to manage your anger; you need to allow the Word of God to direct you in how to conquer it. Anger doesn't have to dominate your life; your home can be free from its devastation, and you can be free from its consequences if you will learn the truths found in this book and follow them. How can you be sure that it will work? Dr. Carter's own experience of overcoming the grip of anger is testimony to the power of God's Word when applied.

Emotional Pain: Wounded, hurt and confused. These words along with many others are used to describe the feelings of emotional pain that afflict so many. The response to these feelings can vary greatly and yet the sad reality is that most of the things we do to cope with our emotional pain only mask it temporarily. This book contains a different kind of answer. The answers here are not to help you cope with your pain, they are to help you eliminate it and experience the healing that you desire. Take the challenge to be brutally honest with yourself and God as you work through these pages and you will find the answer to the peace that you have longed for.

Seizing Triumph from Trials: Do you struggle to get victory over the trials of life? Would you like to know how God's choice ervants found triumph over their trials? Every person goes through trouble, even those who are closest to God, but some let the trials defeat them and some rise up on the trials to find joy and blessings. In <u>Triumph from Trials</u>, author Rick Carter Jr. Ph.D. examines the lives of the great patriarchs Abraham, Isaac, Jacob and Joseph to see how these men of faith responded to trials and what their responses can teach us about how to face the trials of life. It has been said that everyone is entering, going through, or just leaving a trial, but how we respond to them will determine our future. By learning the lessons contained in the lives of these men, you can seize triumph from the trials of life.

These and other books can be ordered at www.ibadirect.com.